CRAVE
VANCOUVER

The Urban Girl's Manifesto

Melody Biringer

1

Welcome to Crave Vancouver

CRAVE Vancouver is more than a guidebook. It's about more than where-to-go and what-to-do. It contains more than basic information. CRAVE Vancouver is a savvy, quality-of-lifestyle book devoted entirely to the best local businesses, owned by women. Featuring over 100 spots and women you need to know in town, CRAVE Vancouver directs you to top boutiques, spas, cafes, stylists, fitness studios, and more, and will introduce you to the inspired, dedicated women behind these exceptional enterprises. At these locales, creativity, quality, innovation, and customer service are paramount. Not only is CRAVE Vancouver an intelligent guidebook for those wanting to know what's happening throughout town, it's a directory for those who recognize, and value the contributions that spirited businesswomen make to our city.

The Urban Girl's Manifesto

We CRAVE Community.
At CRAVE Vancouver we believe in acknowledging, celebrating, and passionately supporting local businesses. We know that when encouraged to thrive, neighbourhood establishments enhance communities. These businesses are original and quirky, and provide rich experiences not usually encountered in mass-market. At CRAVE Vancouver we also know that savvy women are interested in more than mindlessly spending money on shoes, facials, and sweet treats, so we've included the profiles of 100+ local business women to educate, and inspire your own inner entrepreneur.

We CRAVE Adventure.
We could all use a getaway, and at CRAVE Vancouver we believe that you don't need to be a jet setter to have a little adventure. There's so much to explore right here. We encourage you to break your routine, to venture from your regular haunts, to visit new businesses, to explore all the funky finds, and surprising spots that our splendid city has to offer. Whether it's to hunt for a birthday gift, indulge in a spa treatment, order a bouquet of flowers, or connect with like-minded people, let CRAVE Vancouver be your map for a one-of-a-kind, custom hometown journey.

We CRAVE Quality.
At CRAVE Vancouver we know that a satisfying shopping trip requires more than a simple exchange of money for goods, and that a rejuvenating spa date entails more than a quick clip of the cuticles, and a swipe of polish. We know that you value quality and thoughtful service. We know you want to come away with more than a new dress or French manicure. You want to come away feeling uplifted, beautiful, excited, relaxed, and relieved knowing you got the most bang for your buck. We have scoured the city so that you will never be disappointed. In CRAVE Vancouver you will find hidden gems, and old standbys all with one thing in common: they are the best of the best!

What is the best gym or fitness club?

Rumour has it that sex is a great work out. That is, if one applies herself adventurously.

Babs Lucas, Babs Studio Boutique

Absolute Spa Group
Academy of Floral Design
 & New Westminster
 Floral Company
Adhesif Clothing Co.
Alarte Silks
Babs Studio Boutique
Backbone Systems
Bare Basics
Beautybar
The BeautyInk Gallery
Bella Ceramica
Beverly's The Spa on 4th
Bloom Essentials
Blue Ruby Jewellery

Academy of Floral Design & New
Westminster Floral Company

5

Wendy
Lisogar-Cocchia

Q and A

What are the most popular or best
selling products or services?
Organics Spa Binge shea butter body
creme in Rare White Grapefruit.

Who is your role model or mentor?
Peter Legge, President and CEO of
Canada Wide Magazines, and an
international motivation speaker.

Where is your favourite place
to go with your girlfriends?
To the West Vancouver Seawall
with Pamela Martin and our dogs!

What was the motivation behind
starting your business?
Taking care of people. Making
them feel better, healthier,
and more relaxed.

Absolute Pure Relaxation.
Absolute Spa is Canada's largest and most
prestigious spa chain, winning over 36
industry awards, and catering to celebrity
clientele such as Megan Fox, Christina
Aguilera, Stedman Graham, Will Ferrell, and Elle
McPherson. Owner Wendy Lisogar-Cocchia
is lauded as a spa maven for celebrities,
and pampering the stars. Absolute Spa
always delivers the red carpet treatment.

ABSOLUTE SPA GROUP

Pamper

Visit website for locations
604.684.2775
absolutespa.com

Q and A

People may be surprised to know...
That our flower shop is a bona
fide training school under PCTIA,
and all our staff are graduates.

What was the inspiration behind
starting your business?
This school is a dream come true for
us. Watching our students blossom
as they master the art of floral
design, is one of our biggest thrills
at the academy. The long line-up
of clocks acknowledging the home
countries of students from around
the world, bears testament to the
far-reaching impact these classes
carry as the students graduate and
return home with their new skills.

Who is your role model or mentor?
Hitomi Gilliam, a local, award-
winning florist, recognized worldwide as a designer extraordinaire.

Beverley Woodburn
and Daryle Massen

Passionate. Innovative. Encouraging.
Academy of Floral Design and New Westminster
Floral Company is one of Vancouver's best-
kept secrets. This gem is nestled in historic
Sapperton of New Westminster, across from the
Royal Columbian Hospital. Exceptional floral
design, unique gift ideas, and a dedication to
serving their clientele, owners Daryle Massen
and Beverley Woodburn offer training in the
floral arts and the business of floristry, while
providing a working model of a busy flower shop
for their students to observe while they study.

ACADEMY OF FLORAL DESIGN & NEW WESTMINSTER FLORAL COMPANY

Floral

335 E Columbia St, New Westminster
604.525.5819
learn-flower-design.com

9

ADHESIF CLOTHING CO.

Fashion

#418-119 W Pender, Vancouver (by appointment)
778.231.4930
adhesifclothing.com

Eclectic. Bold. Expressive.

Adhesif Clothing Co. uses new and recycled textiles to create noticeable, original, one-of-a-kind garments. This way, every garment retains its very own unique personality, just like you! Adhesif clothing is as unique as the people who are drawn to it.

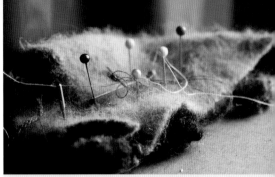

 Q and A

What are the most popular or best selling products or services?
Our one-of-a-kind line of knitwear, comprised of high-quality, recycled wool knits.

People may be surprised to know...
That I am a self-taught designer.

What was the motivation behind starting your business?
My love for vintage clothing, as well as our Mother Earth.

How do you spend your free time?
Contemplating the universe.

What mistake have you made in your business that you will not repeat?
Working ridiculously excessive hours at what I do, without giving myself time to recharge the batteries.

Melissa Ferreira

Q and A

What are the most popular or best selling products or services?
Hand-painted and hand-pleated shibori shawls.

People may be surprised to know...
Everything is done on the premises.

What was the motivation behind starting your business?
Making the world a more colourful place!

What is your indulgence?
Sailing around the world.

Where is the best place to get a manicure?
Most of the time my hands are stained with dyes. Usually I am happy just to scrub them clean! But for a real treat, I have my manicure done at Linda's Urban Spa.

Izabela Sauer

Contemporary Personal Adornment.
In Alarte Silks studio/gallery on Granville Island, Izabela Sauer creates one-of-a-kind, hand-painted, hand-pleated silks, from delicate chiffons, to luminous satins and jacquards. Her custom-made wearable art, scarves, shawls, and wraps are rich in variation and colour. They yield intentions of a woman with a lively personality, who frees herself from every kind of obstacle to be able to trot from one end of the world to the other.

ALARTE SILKS

Fashion

1369 Railspur Alley, Vancouver
778.370.4304
alartesilks.com

13

Q and A

People may be surprised to know...
We are one of the only boutiques
in Canada that caters to women
of all ages and shapes, while
maintaining a polyester-free zone.

Where is your favourite place
to go with your girlfriends?
Seattle. There are real,
HOT men there!

What mistake have you made in your
business that you will not repeat?
There have been few, but I think
that last year, I spent far too
much money on advertising
that never seemed to work.

What are the most popular or
best selling products or services?
Every woman that comes into our
boutique has different needs, a
different shape, and a unique style.
We cater to making each woman
dress and look her absolute best.

Babs Lucas

Sophisticated. Canadian-Made. Worldly.
Babs Studio Boutique caters to women with
life experience in search of edgy, sophisticated
designs available in real women's sizes. The all-
women store (sizes 2-26), carries six exclusive
collections from all over Canada, including the
Babs label that is primarily influenced by exotic
cultures. Babs Lucas's use of stunning natural
fabrics such as bamboo, silk, linen, and organic
jerseys, combined with a deep understanding of
women's shapes, makes Babs boutique a must-
stop-shop, for women with discerning taste.

14

BABS STUDIO BOUTIQUE

Fashion

2410 Granville St, Vancouver
604.408.4881
babs.ca

15

BACKBONE SYSTEMS

Technology

#1318-1030 W Georgia St, Vancouver
604.629.5538
backbonesystems.ca

Effective. Uncomplicated. Fabulous.
Backbone Systems hosts IT for small and medium sized companies. They focus on your IT so you don't have to, and they'll be the backbone of your business, if you like! Backbone can provide all of your IT needs including email and system backup, and can have you working from anywhere in the world, effectively and efficiently. You pay one monthly fee that includes all the IT help you'll ever need.

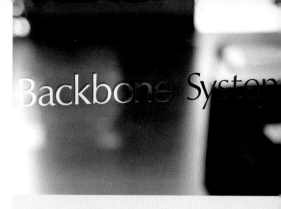

Backbone System

Q and A

People may be surprised to know...
IT is not that complicated
when it works correctly.

What was the motivation behind starting your business?
Seeing geeks confuse
people needlessly.

Who is your role model or mentor?
A cross between Madonna
and Bill Gates!

How do you spend your free time?
A cocktail in one hand, and
my blackberry in the other.

What is your indulgence?
Travelling, as much as possible.

Where is your favourite place
to go with your girlfriends?
Down to the local pub.

Sarah Morton

ckBerry
ution Provider
iance Member

que acknowledges your partnership with
In Motion (RIM) through your
tion in the BlackBerry® Alliance Program.

BlackBerry.
Alliance Member

17

BARE BASICS
LINGERIE

Fashion

4431 W 10th Ave, Vancouver
604.224.3777
barebasicslingerie.com

What are the most popular or best selling products or services?
Chantelle, Prima Donna, Empreinte, Hanky Panky, Frou Frou.

People may be surprised to know...
Your bra should be hand-washed after every wear. The more often you wash it, the longer it will last.

What was the motivation behind starting your business?
I grew up in and around the lingerie business. When I was 11, my Mom opened the first Bare Basics store in Steveston.

What is your indulgence?
Shopping, wine, and Vegas!

Where is your favourite place to go with your girlfriends?
Any of our houses, where we can sit back and relax.

Intimate. Knowledgeable. Friendly.
Known for specialising in bra fittings for over 23 years, Bare Basics caters to the lingerie needs of women of all shapes and sizes. What makes Bare Basics so unique? It's all about the fitters. With combined experience of over 100 years, the Bare Basics staff is professionally trained to address all your questions and concerns, to find the perfect garment that suits your style.

Nicole
Hosein

19

Q and A

People may be surprised to know...
We offer makeup lessons,
which are very popular!

What was the motivation behind starting your business?
I wanted to create an environment that was welcoming, where you didn't have to feel intimidated to ask questions or try products. A place that offers amazing, elusive brands.

What is your indulgence?
Trying out new products.

Where is your favourite place to go with your girlfriends?
New York.

What are the most popular or best selling products or services?
Makeup in particular, but everything is a hit!

Tasleem Suleman

Vibrant. Enticing. Playful.

Beautybar is a fresh, funky, ultra-hip, beauty haven offering the finest, most coveted, innovative beauty and self-care products from around the globe, with a distinct emphasis on quality, lasting appeal, and service-service-service! Trendsetters and beauty mavens alike will find a welcoming and dynamic shopping experience where hands-on play is encouraged. The atmosphere is intoxicating with vivacious scents of exotic lotions and potions, and the rainbow palette of lipsticks, glosses, and so much more. Beautybar offers beauty for everyone, man or woman, inside and out.

VINCENT LONGO

BEAUTYBAR

Pamper

2142 W 4th Ave, Vancouver
604.733.9000
beautybarcosmetics.com

THE BEAUTYINK GALLERY

Pamper

#101-1529 W 6th Ave, Vancouver
604.639.3609
beautyink.ca

22

Elegant. Progressive. Exclusive.
The BeautyInk Gallery is Vancouver's exclusive makeup service boutique, specialising in permanent cosmetics, semi-permanent lashes, weddings, airbrush, and makeup effects. Owner Shauna Magrath customizes all services for every individual, and books by appointment only for the best possible results!

Q and A

What are the most popular or best selling products or services?
Permanent cosmetics are the most popular service we provide.

People may be surprised to know...
That I have 15 years of experience working with Hollywood's elite in the film industry, and have worked for every major studio in Hollywood.

What mistake have you made in your business that you will not repeat?
Always taking peoples advice. Do your homework, and follow your gut!

What is your indulgence?
Massages, pedicures, anything to pamper myself, including great food.

Where is your favourite place to go with your girlfriends?
A girls' night out dinner, drinks, and dancing.

Shauna Magrath

BELLA CERAMICA

Lifestyle

1381 Marine Dr, Second Floor, West Vancouver
604.925.3115
bellaceramicastudio.com

Relaxing. Fun. Creative.
Bella Ceramica is a paint-your-own-pottery studio, where customers can walk in anytime to relax and let their creative juices flow. With 2000 square feet of open space, and a close view of the water, it is also a perfect place for parties, showers, and gatherings. Bella Ceramica offers more than just ceramics; they also provide workshops for mosaics and glass fusing.

What are the most popular or best selling products or services?
A personalized gift of art, created by you.

People may be surprised to know...
Drop in anytime! No appointment is necessary.

What was the motivation behind starting your business?
Painting pottery is cheaper than therapy, and a lot more fun.

What is your indulgence?
Bubble baths, chocolate, and Frappuccinos.

How do you spend your free time?
Painting!

Where is your favourite place to go with your girlfriends?
Shopping together is so much fun.

Mimie
Lee

25

BEVERLY'S THE SPA ON 4TH

Pamper

2185 W 4th Ave, Vancouver
604.732.4402
spaon4th.com

Friendly. Professional. Skilled.

Beverly's is Kitsilano's favourite neighbourhood day spa. Owner Anne Lauener consistently provides top-quality, innovative treatments, advanced products, and legendary service. Beverly's is a team of friendly professionals dedicated to providing you with a memorable experience. Their goal is that you leave the spa feeling cared for, informed, and happy with how you look and feel - every time you visit!

Q and A

People may be surprised to know... After 26 years, we now span over 4,000 square feet on three levels! To meet client demand, we have expanded four times in 12 years, yet still maintain our boutique feel and attention to providing a personal experience.

Who is your role model or mentor? Jane Wurwand. The Founder and Owner of Dermalogica and The International Dermal Institute.

Where is the best place to find gifts? Paboom in Kits. They have a good selection of frames, candles and different household hostess gift items, that are also well priced.

How do you spend your free time? Run, row, blade, ski, pilates, yoga French, leadership and meditation courses, entertaining, movies, and spa time!

Anne Lauener

27

Q and A

What are the most popular or best selling products or services?
Our Picasso Pedicures originally made us famous in Vancouver and they remain the most popular service we offer.

Who is your role model or mentor?
All women we meet with their own companies give something to us. We don't have just one in particular.

What mistake have you made in your business that you will not repeat?
Underestimating ourselves.

What is the best gym or fitness club?
The whole city is our gym. Why be inside when you can be outside?!

What is your indulgence?
Trying to take time for ourselves. Emphasis on "trying"!

Kimberly and Nicole Critten

Fun! Fun! Fun!

At Bloom Essentials, Nicole and Kimberly Critten try their best to make each and every spa visit a little escape from the day-to-day madness of life. New and old friends alike will feel right at home in their relaxed, casual atmosphere. If you appreciate over-the-top customer service, back-to-basics treatments, a knowledgeable staff, and a welcoming space, then you'll get along just fine!

BLOOM ESSENTIALS

Pamper

#3-1854 W 1st Ave, Vancouver
604.736.8960
bloomessentials.com

BLUE RUBY JEWELLERY

Jewellery

1089 Robson St, Vancouver
604.899.2583

Oakridge Centre
#437-650 W 41st Ave, Vancouver
604.269.2583

2125 W 41st Ave, Vancouver
604.266.9117

6551 #3 Road, Richmond
604.247.2583

Pacific Centre
#51D-701 W Georgia St, Vancouver
604.693.3118

Metropolis at Metrotown
#2176-4700 Kingsway, Burnaby
604.454.9334

945 Park Royal South, West Vancouver
604.913.3118

blueruby.com

Vibrant. Modern. Glamourous.

Blue Ruby is Vancouver's original jewellery boutique, with seven locations throughout the Lower Mainland. Established in 1998, Blue Ruby showcases both local and international designers, and is the first choice for Vancouver's discerning trend setters. With our signature "Beauty Bar" boutiques modeled after Elizabeth Arden's 1940's boutique in New York City, Blue Ruby is an experience of luxury and indulgence.

Q and A

What mistake have you made in your business that you will not repeat?
Mistakes are a valuable tool and will always occur. Don't be afraid of them but instead study and learn from them.

Where is the best place to find gifts?
Where you'd least expect it. The key to a good gift is to buy something that the recipient wouldn't otherwise buy for themselves.

People may be surprised to know...
I sleepwalk on most nights.

What is the best gym or fitness club?
Any of the beaches in our beautiful city!

Who is your role model or mentor?
My family is involved in retail and they have provided invaluable advice that you just wouldn't get from other people.

Nancy Hill

31

What is your indulgence?

"*My indulgence is shoes. I buy them faster than I can wear them!*"

Susan Vu, Boudoir

Bodacious Lifestyles
Boudoir
Breathe Spa
Bruce Eyewear
Burlesque Beauties
Butter Baked Goods
The Campoverde Social Club
Carrie & Danielle
Changes Clothing &
   Jewellery Bar
Chick Pea
Colektiv Images
Country Beads
The Cross Decor & Design

Butter Baked Goods

Q and A

What are the most popular or best selling products or services?
Dresses, tops, athletic wear, jeans, and accessories.

What mistake have you made in your business that you will not repeat?
Learn more about bookkeeping in the beginning.

How do you spend your free time?
Singing, swimming, sailing, walking, taking pictures.

Where is your favourite place to go with your girlfriends?
The Jam at the Railway on a Saturday afternoon.

What is the best gym or fitness club?
Kits pool rocks in the summer. Queen Elizabeth park in the fall and winter for walk/runs.

Fun. Inspirational. Friendly.
Celebrate your curves at Bodacious! Owners Lorna Ketler and Barb Wilkins feature locally designed clothing and accessories that fit and flatter your curvy figure (sizes 10-24). Bodacious features sexy dresses, flirty skirts, funky tees, comfy athletic wear, and accessories. Bring your girlfriends for a fun and supportive shopping experience.

Lorna Ketler and Barb Wilkins

BODACIOUS
LIFESTYLES

Fashion

4393 Main St, Vancouver
604.874.2811
bodacious.ca

35

Q and A

What are the most popular or best selling products or services?
Dresses have become a Boudoir staple. Chic day dresses, fabulous party dresses, pretty evening dresses - we've got the full range.

What was the motivation behind starting your business?
Creative freedom. I wanted to be in an environment that would creatively inspire me, keep me fresh and keep me growing.

How do you spend your free time?
I spend most of my free time catching up with friends and family.

Where is your favourite place to go with your girlfriends?
We don't have a favourite, but we love trying out new restaurants around the city.

Susan Vu

Pretty. Intimate. Chic.
Boudoir is bringing pretty back. Tucked away in Vancouver's trendy Yaletown is a coveted wardrobe for the ultimate feminista. Whether you need to look fabulously stylish for a night out with the girls, effortlessly sexy for your Wednesday night date, or simply flawless for the big event of the season, you'll be sure to find something pretty to wear in this ultra-chic closet. The best part? There's a good chance the girl you love to hate won't be wearing the same thing.

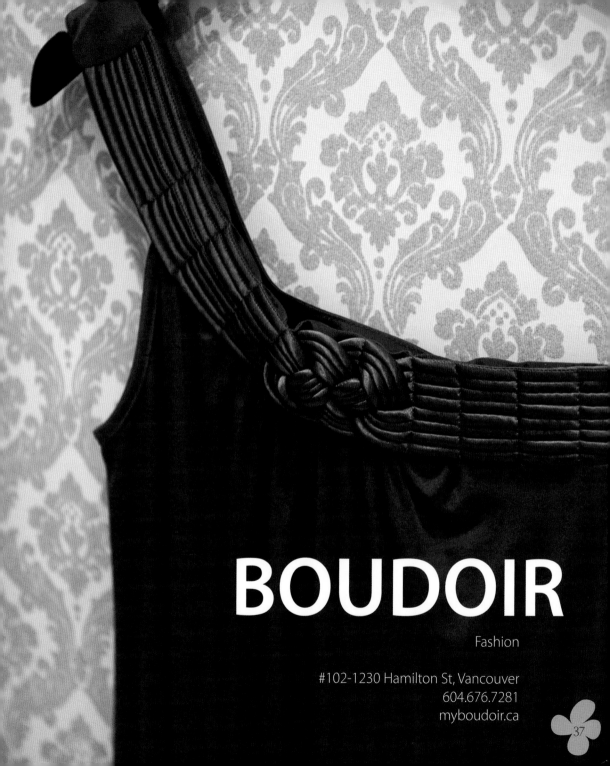

BOUDOIR

Fashion

#102-1230 Hamilton St, Vancouver
604.676.7281
myboudoir.ca

BREATHE SPA

Pamper

464 Granville St, Vancouver
604.688.4769
breathespa.net

Relaxed. Intimate. Quality.
Breathe Spa is an exclusive boutique spa in the heart of downtown Vancouver, offering only the highest quality skin and body care services and products, within a beautiful and relaxed setting. Breathe Spa has been recognized as one of the top spas in Vancouver for its excellent quality service and attention to detail.

People may be surprised to know... I met my husband at a Halloween party on a cruise ship, in the middle of a hurricane whilst crossing the Atlantic.

What was the motivation behind starting your business?
To create the spa that I always wanted to go to but could never find.

What mistake have you made in your business that you will not repeat?
I believe life is a journey and mistakes are merely stepping stones disguised as the perfect opportunity.

What are the most popular or best selling products or services?
Our signature service is our amazing two-hour facial, and our most popular product is our Vivier high potency serum.

Victoria Carr

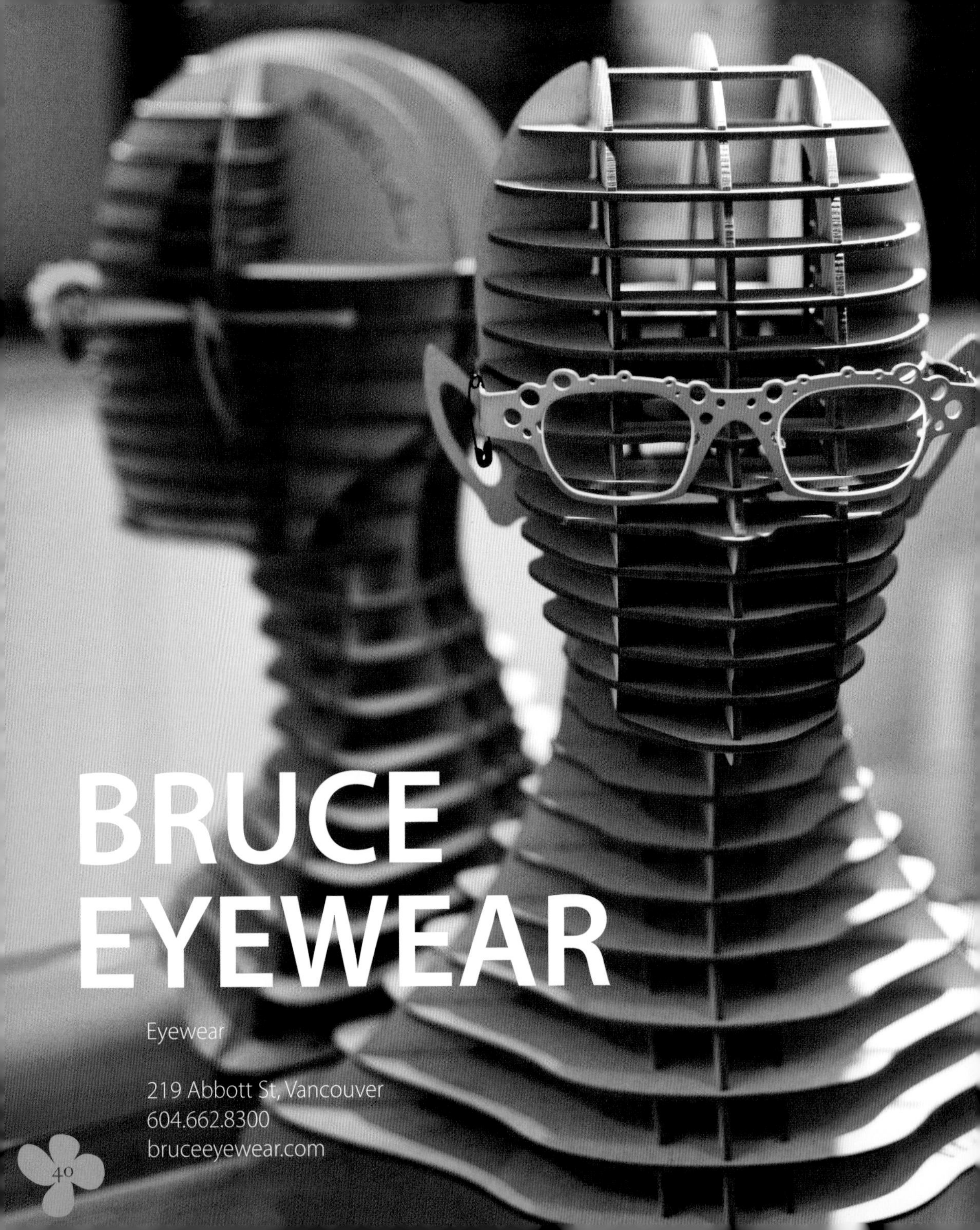

BRUCE
EYEWEAR

Eyewear

219 Abbott St, Vancouver
604.662.8300
bruceeyewear.com

40

Welcoming. Helpful. Exceptional.
Bruce Eyewear has been helping people look
fabulous in eyeglasses for over eight years.
Their beautifully curated frame collections
are eclectic and seriously chic, with many
lines unique to their Gastown shop. Bruce
Eyewear also specializes in state-of-the-art
lenses, and non-prescription sunglasses.

Nada Vuksic

Q and A

What was the motivation behind
starting your business?
Independence and the desire to
eliminate the "orthopedic shoe"
attitude towards eyeglasses.

Who is your role model or mentor?
My mother, the finest person I
have ever known, with a great
sense of style and absolute
integrity in all things.

What mistake have you made in your
business that you will not repeat?
Any occasion where I did not
absolutely trust my instincts.

Where is your favourite place
to go with your girlfriends?
For a pedicure, out for dinner,
and shopping, of course!

BURLESQUE BEAUTIES

Fitness

Visit website for nearest location
604.537.8590
burlesquebeauties.com

42

Classy. Entertaining. Professional.

The six sassy, sexy ladies of Burlesque Beauties want you to take a look at the world of "Nouveau Burlesque." Their professional live and interactive cabaret dance show is filled with sex appeal, humor, class, and talent. Participate in their dance classes, which are offered to women looking to have fun, keep in shape, and dance like a classy, sexy, and confident woman.

Q and A

What mistake have you made in your business that you will not repeat? Follow your instincts; they are always right! Master and learn how to balance your personal and professional careers. I love what I do with every ounce of my heart, but I try not to lose myself in it. Always remember you are a separate person and entity outside of your business.

People may be surprised to know... It all started out as a bunch of friends who just wanted to have fun and do a burlesque-style dance performance at a friend's fundraiser over four years ago.

How do you spend your free time? I really enjoy yoga and pilates, spending time with my good friends and family, cooking, travelling, and learning about whatever interests me at the moment.

Carla Catherwood

Q and A

What are the most popular or best selling products or services?
The Homemade Oreo is really popular but our marshmallows are making us famous. We make them in a variety of flavours but toasted coconut still continues to be the biggest seller.

People may be surprised to know... Our marshmallows are fat free, wheat free, dairy free, and almost guilt free!

Who is your role model or mentor?
Anyone who has been brave enough to leave a secure and comfortable career to follow a dream and role the dice. Ina Garten is great example.

What mistake have you made in your business that you will not repeat?
Letting my head convince my gut it is wrong.

Ray Porcellato and Rosie Daykin

Comforting. Friendly. Truly Tasty!
Butter Baked Goods is a family owned and operated bakery located on the West Side of Vancouver. They specialize in nostalgic home baking using only the finest ingredients. There are no additives nor preservatives in their baking, and of course, only real butter! Every day they feature many cookies, bars, cupcakes, homemade marshmallows, pies, scones, muffins, and any other yummy treats they can think up. People have taken such a liking to their food, that they now sell across Canada to many fine retailers.

BUTTER
BAKED GOODS

Eats

4321 Dunbar St, Vancouver
604.221.4333
butterbakedgoods.com

THE CAMPOVERDE SOCIAL CLUB

Networking

1660 Cypress St, Vancouver
604.734.1660
campoverde.ca

46

Sophisticated. Social. Adventurous.
The Campoverde Social Club is
Vancouver's easiest and friendliest way to
expand your social network. Whether for
friendship, love or business, Campoverde
has proven the most successful portal
to a fun, and fulfilling social life.

 Q and A

What are the most popular or best
selling products or services?
Nightly events, delicious food,
and access to interesting,
sophisticated people.

Who is your role model or mentor?
Eleanor Roosevelt.

People may be surprised to know...
That we are exclusive but exceedingly
friendly and down-to-earth.

What was the motivation behind
starting your business?
I had moved back to Vancouver after
living in Madrid, London, Paris, and
New York, and found that Vancouver
was a difficult city in which to make
friends and build a social network.

How do you spend your free time?
Travelling, skiing, reading, doing
yoga, visiting with friends.

Rachel Greenfeld

Carrie McCarthy
and Danielle LaPorte

Q and A

What was the inspiration behind starting your business?
We wanted to create beauty and meaning in every way possible. Creative freedom, financial freedom, loving relationships - it's all possible.

Where is the best place to buy shoes?
Gravity Pope on 4th. No question about it. Holt Renfrew is also great.

What mistake have you made in your business that you will not repeat?
If you don't follow your deeper instincts in terms of business partnerships - it usually leads to hard feelings. Intuition is Queen.

How do you spend your free time?
Vocation and home blend for us. We're always hunting, always strategising, always looking for the truth within a person or a painting.

Meaningful. Powerful. Creative.
Deemed "Missionaries for self expression," Carrie and Danielle are the creators of the Style Statement - the two words that name your true self. Their bestselling book, *Style Statement: Live By Your Own Design* is a discover-it-yourself workbook for creating your own personal Style Statement, which can be used as a touchstone for making more powerful choices in your whole life - from your wardrobe to relationships, career plans to to-do lists. They also offer private, one-on-one Style Statement sessions. Their website is a one-of-a-kind resource for wisdom and how-to's for living an inspired life. Subscribe to their interactive Daily Q&A at CarrieandDanielle.com.

48

CARRIE & DANIELLE

Stylists

604.732.1717
carrieanddanielle.com

Q and A

People may be surprised to know...
How many hours I work in a week
to make Changes great. How many
charities we support monthly and
annually, along with the hundreds
of pieces of clothing we donate
directly to women in need in
Vancouver, despite being "for profit."

Who is your role model or mentor?
My Mom, who owns Changes
in Calgary, is such a hard worker
and a success in everything she
does. She is fearless, fashionable,
generous, assertive, and nurturing.
My dog, Shadow, is also a great
role model as he is happy,
forgiving, patient, and loves
Mother Earth; all the characteristics
everyone should exude.

How do you spend your free time?
Roadtrips, Montana, Kauai,
backpacking, my garden, bakery
cafes, and taking Shadow to the
beach where he is the most happy.

Rhonda Davis

Empowering. Innovative. Generous.
Changes Clothing & Jewellery Bar offers new
and like-new, trends and consigned clothing,
with a jewellery bar that sparkles with designs
by Canadian artists. Owner Rhonda Davis
aims to create a win-win situation for the
community, shoppers, consignors, staff, and
Mother Earth, all while encouraging women
to be empowered. Changes has received the
Vancouver's Best Consignment Store Award
every year since 2002. Change is good!

50

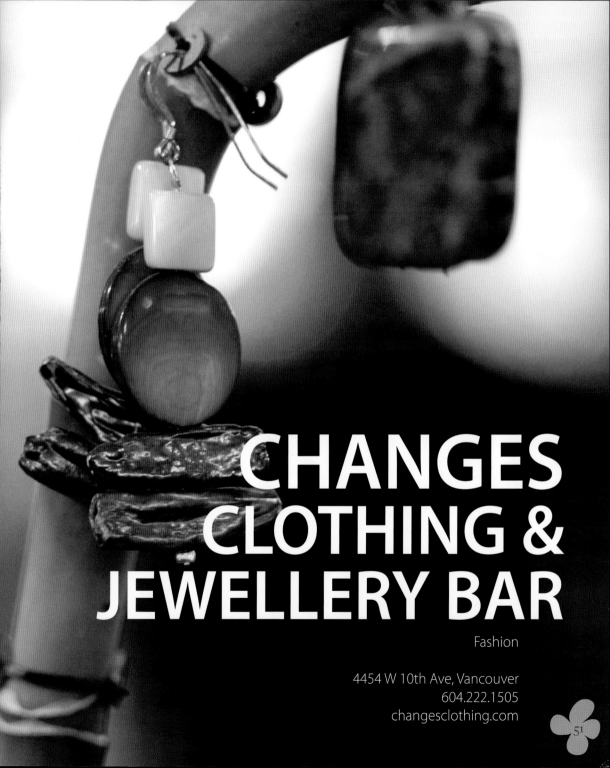

CHANGES CLOTHING & JEWELLERY BAR

Fashion

4454 W 10th Ave, Vancouver
604.222.1505
changesclothing.com

51

Q and A

What was the motivation behind starting your business?
Finding a way to balance motherhood and the passion of doing something we love for a career.

What mistake have you made in your business that you will not repeat?
Thinking that we are able to do it all. Working moms do need extra hands at times.

How do you spend your free time?
Walking with coffee and kids, laughing, chatting, shopping.

What is your indulgence?
Adding the women's section into Chick Pea we are now constantly shopping for ourselves in-store, as we are stocking our very favourite pieces of jewellery, clothing, skin care, and accessories.

Sarah Hoivik and Kim Mathewes

Natural. Fresh. Sophisticated.
Chick Pea is a European-style boutique, full of the things owners Sarah Hoivik and Kim Mathewes love most for babies, toddlers, and moms. You will find a balance of classic charm and urban whimsy in their product lines. An unexpected innocence and quiet energy radiate from the store's white farmhouse tables and brick walls. This ambiance, coupled with a view of the river, creates a safe environment to enjoy a quiet afternoon choosing your very favourite special items to take home.

CHICK PEA

Children's

613 Front St, New Westminster
604.525.2266
chickpeakids.com

53

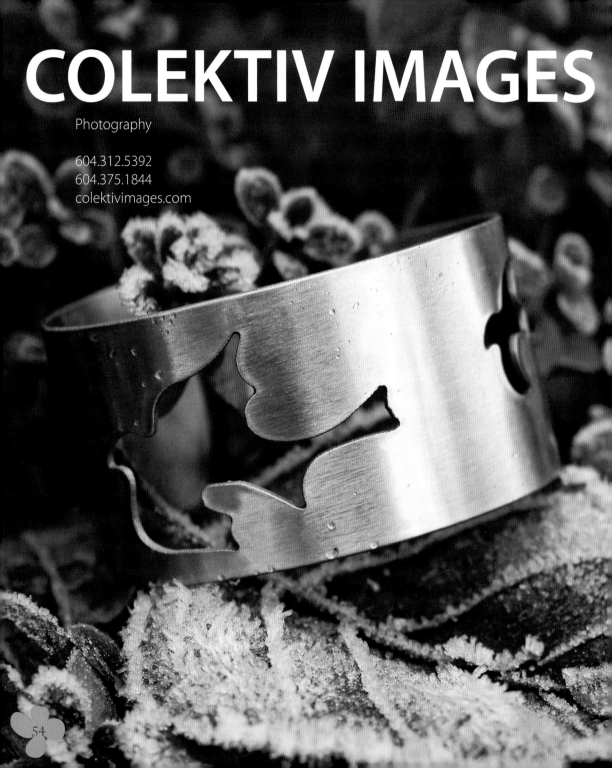

COLEKTIV IMAGES

Photography

604.312.5392
604.375.1844
colektivimages.com

54

Cohesive. Collaborative. Consistent.
First meeting at a professional photography program, Meghan Kirkpatrick and Jessica Offer became close friends who shared the same passion for photography and design. Both wanting to work with, and create unique images for local talent, Coletkiv Images was born. Drawing their creative inspiration from inventive, independent designers in and around Vancouver, and through design concept meetings, they are able to capture the artistic visions of their clients.

What are the most popular or best selling products or services?
Our custom photography packages are most popular because they allow us to suit the individual needs of our clients.

What is your indulgence?
Travelling, dark chocolate, and vintage pieces, old and full of character.

Who is your role model or mentor?
Anahata Katkin, Candice Meyer, and local photographers Reine and Jana for infusing so much art in their photography.

Where is the best place to get a pedicure?
Jessica: He'd kill me if I told you this, but my husband does an immaculate job.

Meghan Kirkpatrick
and Jessica Offer

COUNTRY BEADS

Lifestyle

2015 W 4th Ave, Vancouver
604.730.8056
countrybeads.com

Dazzling. Creative. Fashionable.

Country Beads is a unique bead store offering all you need to create all the latest styles. They specialize in a diverse selection of semi-precious stones (including exceptional one-of-a-kind hand-cut pieces), along with FW pearls, crystal, wood, glass, and more! Also available is sterling silver, vermeil and gold-fill findings, and chain by-the-foot for your quality piece of jewellery. Beautiful beads, excellent customer service, and a cozy atmosphere makes shopping at Country Beads an experience not to be missed.

 Q and A

Sue Gill

People may be surprised to know...
How many incredibly beautiful semi-precious stones we have!

Who is your role model or mentor?
All the women I meet who have managed to find a balance between work-life and family-life.

How do you spend your free time?
Gardening, cooking, playing with my two young children, doing anything outside.

What was the inspiration behind starting your business?
Making an interesting space with spectacular products and service, helping people create their own beaded jewellery.

What is your indulgence?
Good food, really good wine, and the occasional spa treatment.

Q and A

What are the most popular or best selling products or services?
Custom-designed cushions and pillows, wallpaper, and chandeliers

People may be surprised to know...
We still get a thrill when we see someone carrying a "Cross" shopping bag! We inwardly hope they enjoyed their shopping experience.

What was the inspiration behind starting your business?
To become a resource for classic and beautiful furnishings and accessories, and to bring the best design trends to Vancouver that the world has to offer, with a strong focus on superior customer service.

Where is your favourite place to go with your girlfriends?
Cooking and entertaining for friends at home.

Darci Ilich and
Stephanie Vogler

Elegant. Progressive. Sophisticated.
The Cross brings a new style to Vancouver that is often seen in European homes and magazines -- a relaxed feeling, complimented with beautifully appointed, luxury items and found objects, sexy antiques, and exquisite furnishings. From bedding to bath, sofas to scented candles, ribbons to wrap, The Cross has all of the elements required for a lifetime of style and beauty.

THE CROSS
DECOR & DESIGN

Lifestyle

1198 Homer St, Vancouver
604.689.2900
thecrossdesign.com

59

*Where is your favourite place
to go with your girlfriends?*

"*A place where we could
dance. I also love to
shop with other women.
I value the female ritual.*"

Edie Orenstein, Edie Hats

Daily Dose Media
Della Optique
Designhouse
Domo Tea
Dorothy Grant
Dream Apparel and Articles
 for People
Dream Designs
Edie Hats
Elements Wellness Centre
Emelle's Catering
Enda B Men & Women
Escents Aromatherapy
EvelineCharles Salons & Spas

DAILY DOSE
MEDIA INC.

Media

778.329.6190
vitaminv.ca

Sarah Bancroft
and Tara Parker Tait

Irreverent. Clever. Worldly.

Daily Dose Media is the publisher of savvy,
online, style supplements in major Canadian
cities that target educated, fun-loving women
who are starved for time and hungry for
information. Dispensing short, daily, good-
for-you style vitamins on topics such as
Fashion, Health, Beauty, Home, Culture and
Dining, that are timely and relevant, Vitamin
V is the first thing you read in the morning
(after the ingredients on the cereal box).

What are the most popular or best
selling products or services?
Our daily doses are free, and we
find Fashion is our most popular
topic. Restaurants, books and films
get searched most in our archives.
And whenever we publish a joke,
it gets passed around like crazy.

People may be surprised to know...
We visit and test everything we write
about in person (even if it means
wearing a hard hat) to provide the
most accurate coverage possible.
For everything we cover, we test at
least a dozen places and products
that don't make the grade.

Who is your role model or mentor?
Trailblazers like Martha Stewart,
Barbara Walters, Madonna.
They've paved the way for
women everywhere.

DELLA OPTIQUE

Eyewear

2589 W Broadway, Vancouver
604.742.3937
dellaoptique.com

Chic. Fun. Unique.

Remaining at the forefront of the latest eyewear and sunglass trends, Della Optique's discerning staff provide expert assistance in selection from an extensive collection of unique designer eyewear and sunglasses. Glasses are a fashion accessory and reflect your personality. Getting new glasses or taking care of your eyes should be a fun experience. Della Optique's clients definitely leave thinking, "EYE LOVE IT!"

DELLA OPTIQUE
Visioncare + Eyewear

Della Chow

Q and A

What was the inspiration behind starting your business?
My family owned a restaurant. I wanted to provide that same type of friendly service and environment to clients who needed glasses.

Who is your role model or mentor?
My role model is a clothing designer, Rozemerie Cuevas of JC Studio, a boutique clothing studio where clients get concierge service when they see her for clothing.

What are the most popular or best selling products or services?
Sunglasses and funky eyewear.

What mistake have you made in your business that you will not repeat?
Trying to have a paperless office.

How do you spend your free time?
Cleaning my house... it is a never ending process!

DESIGNHOUSE

Lifestyle

1110 Mainland St, Vancouver
604.681.2800
designhouse.ca

Modern. Friendly. Urban.
Designhouse owners Anne and Steve Miller believe good design should be available to everyone. This is why they offer great, modern design that is functional, good-looking, and well-priced, in a friendly, no-pressure atmosphere. Lines like Alessi, Bludot, Calligaris, DelaEspada, Iittala, Kartell, Magis, Marimekko, Kate and Jack Spade, and many more are featured. Designhouse also sells its own custom furniture.

Q and A

What are the most popular or best selling products or services?
Sofas, dining tables, beds, bags, and glassware.

People may be surprised to know...
We design and build our own furniture.

What was the motivation behind starting your business?
Offering good design to everyone, without any pretension.

What mistake have you made in your business that you will not repeat?
Underestimating the value of working with suppliers that place their trust in you, and support you in promoting their products.

How do you spend your free time?
Visiting my family and travelling.

Where is the best place to find gifts?
Yaletown and places I travel to.

Anne Miller

Q and A

What are the most popular or best selling products or services?
"Vanilla Cloud" flavour-infused Matcha.

People may be surprised to know...
Anne: Domo flavoured matcha goes great with alcohol and it's only 20 calories per serving! Tammy: That matcha is the healthiest tea you can get, and we make it taste great. Matcha can be more than you think!

What is your indulgence?
Anne: Drinking cucumber water martinis in the shower. Tammy: A long bath with a gossip magazine.

Where is the best place to get a pedicure?
Anne: Shanghai. They soak your feet in this magic rice water that leaves your skin so soft, and massage your feet for a full hour. All for $5. Tammy: Spa Utopia - it's like walking into another world!

Well-balanced. Fun-loving. Foward-reaching. Tammy Olsson and Anne Yeo are committed to reinventing tea, by fusing its traditional, therapeutic qualities with fresh ideas and flavours. They blend the old with new to create a unique tea experience. Domo Tea is a small, sassy company with a big heart, lots of grand ambitions, and the drive to achieve them. Their tea can be found all over Canada, and shortly, the US.

Tammy Olsson and Anne Yeo

DOMO TEA

Eats

2115 Columbia St, Vancouver
604.809.9009
domotea.com

domo

ginger kiss
matcha

Q and A

People may be surprised to know...
We cut each garment one at a time,
and sew them in our own facility.

What was the inspiration behind
starting your business?
The need to show our
art on clothing, in a very
contemporary fashion.

What is your indulgence?
Cooking great Italian
recipes on a Sunday.

What mistake have you made in your
business that you will not repeat?
Listening to the wrong advice
from people who do not
understand your business.

How do you spend your free time?
I like to read, exercise, and enjoy
long hikes and walks on the beach.

Dorothy Grant

Quality. Art. Service.
Dorothy Grant is Canada's Premier First Nations
designer. Her clothing and accessories line
features precision-cut, Haida artwork on
the best natural fabrics available. Her studio
and store focus on customer service, and
made-to-measure garments. Dorothy Grant
black label, DYG sport label, and Grant's
award-winning, high-end wearable art
line, FeastWear, can be found in museum
gift stores in Canada and the USA.

DOROTHY GRANT

Fashion

138 W 6th Ave, Vancouver
604.681.0201
dorothygrant.com

Q and A

People may be surprised to know...
That we've been around for 15 years!

What was the motivation behind starting your business?
I needed a place to sell what I make, and Vancouver designers needed a place that understands them and would take a chance on new ideas.

What mistake have you made in your business that you will not repeat?
I will never open a business when I'm 25 again. I think I'll travel more first.

How do you spend your free time?
What free time? I have a son who is five, a husband who is not, and a house that is 100, never mind owning a business! Sleeping is how I spend my free time!

What is your indulgence?
Shoes, shopping, and chocolate.

Wendy de Kruyff

Stylish. Relaxed. Nice.
Established in 1993, Dream Apparel and Articles for People has represented many of Vancouver's talented designers for the past 15 years! Owner Wendy de Kruyff offers clothing, jewellery, bags, and many other hand-crafted items. Sometimes trendy, sometimes classic, Dream style is always unique.

DREAM APPAREL AND ARTICLES FOR PEOPLE

Fashion

311 W Cordova St, Vancouver
604.683.7326

The Netloft, Granville Island, Vancouver

dreamvancouver.com

DREAM DESIGNS

Lifestyle

956 Commercial Dr, Vancouver
604.254.5012
dreamdesigns.ca

74

Natural. Sustainable. Stylish.

Founded in 1981, Dream Designs is Vancouver's leading green lifestyle business, featuring stylish bedding, bath, yoga, and baby products, plus clothing that is locally made, fair-trade, ecological, and sustainable. Dream Designs currently has two stores, one on the diverse and vibrant Commercial Drive, and the other one at the newly constructed sustainable building complex at Lynn Valley Town Centre in North Vancouver.

Q and A

What are the most popular or best selling products or services?
Organic and natural bedding, soy clothing, hemp shower curtains.

What mistake have you made in your business that you will not repeat?
Spending too much time at work. It's all too easy to lose track of time when I am at work. When you own your own business, there is a never ending to-do list. I need to remind myself to take care of my family and personal life, especially now that I am expecting a baby.

How do you spend your free time?
Zen meditation, reading, hiking.

Who is your role model or mentor?
There have been many. I am a listener and observer. There is always something to learn from everyone around me.

Bei Linda Tang

EDIE HATS

Fashion

#4-1666 Johnston St, The Netloft, Granville Island, Vancouver
604.683.4280
ediehats.com

Sensual. Vibrant. Joyous.

Edie Hats is an experiential retail environment that uses the powerful language of fashion and accessories, with hats as the focal point, for a celebration of self-expression. Owner Edie Orenstein has created an atmosphere that is an unforgettable magnet for people from all over the world. The abundance of beautiful, distinctive products, vibrant energy, live music, and theatre productions, creates a warm community atmosphere, where loyal customers return again and again for their hat fix.

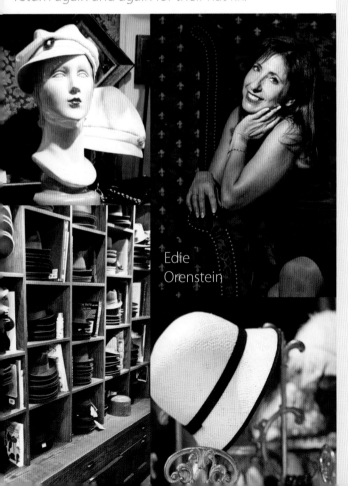

Edie Orenstein

People may be surprised to know...
The store converts into a theatre and performance cafe at night, and re-converts for the morning retail traffic.

What was the inspiration behind starting your business?
I am inspired by almost everything I experience. In starting a business, I had to pick one product and hats seemed to be the most powerful icon that connects history, imagery, and self-expression to the present.

What mistake have you made in your business that you will not repeat?
I believe there are no mistakes, only learning experiences. Which means there are too many to list here.

Who is your role model or mentor?
I have a mentor for everything I have ever been involved in. I gather mentors.

77

Q and A

What are the most popular or best selling products or services?
Acupuncture Facial Rejuvenation is a great alternative to Botox and plastic surgery. It brings beauty and balance together.

People may be surprised to know...
Every destination I travel to, I visit a wellness centre or spa.

What was the inspiration behind starting your business?
My own health issues got me interested in trying acupuncture, and I loved it so much so that I became a registered acupuncturist. Throughout school, I kept visualizing a big, beautiful place where people had various alternative therapies they could choose from to heal naturally.

How do you spend your free time?
I am blessed to live so close to the beach so I get to enjoy walking it with husband and dog.

Kelli Taylor

Healing, Tranquil. Relaxing.
Elements Wellness Centre is located in the heart of Kitsilano in Vancouver. It is a multi-disciplinary centre that brings together a vast variety of different alternative therapies, all in one place. A comfortable, safe healing environment is provided for each client, so they can relax and let their bodies heal naturally.

78

ELEMENTS
WELLNESS CENTRE

Pamper

#207-2678 W Broadway, Vancouver
604.732.9355 (WELL)
elementswellnesscentre.com

Q and A

How do you spend your free time?
Creating in other mediums -
pottery, sewing, and cooking! I
love travelling to explore other
cuisines, and I volunteer.

What are the most popular or best
selling products or services?
Maple mustard wild sockeye salmon,
fresh roasted turkey and cranberry
sandwich, and our famous Friday
Blue Plate, featuring BBQ chicken!

People may be surprised to know...
We are a member of GreenTable
Network, promoting
sustainability in our industry.

Where is the best place
to get a pedicure?
Jo's Toes & Esthetics, because Joanna
Konkin gives me happy feet!

Mary Lee
Newnham

Contemporary. Delectable. Innovative.
Emelle's is a caterer-meets-urban-diner. The café
serves breakfast and lunch, Monday through
Friday, and catering is 24/7. All of their clients
have become dependant on Emelle's to set
the precedent for remarkable service and
delectable cuisine. Whatever the occasion,
owner Mary Lee Newenham's mandate is to
use only the freshest ingredients, and create
a hospitable ambience, because at Emelle's,
they cater to you with ease and grace.

EMELLE'S CATERING

Eats, Event Services

177 W 7th Ave, Vancouver
604.875.6551
emelles.com

Yvonne
Leung-Kwan

Q and A

People may be surprised to know...
I am a true core workaholic, who will
never miss a single day of work.

Who is your role model or mentor?
My grand aunt, as she always
remained so well-poised and positive,
regardless of the circumstances.

What mistake have you made in your
business that you will not repeat?
I neglected myself, always
putting others first.

How do you spend your free time?
I dabble with colours and
do acrylic painting.

What was the motivation behind
starting your business?
My husband wanted me to do
something that would give me the
flexibility to balance my family and
career. Being my own boss was the
best option at that time.

Retail-Therapy. Fashion-Forward.
Exhilarating Experience.
Enda B Men & Women has been an iconic
fashion store in the heart of Point Grey Village
since the store's inception, over 25 years ago.
The strong clientele with loyal and repeat
customers, is an integral part of Enda B's success.
Today, Enda B continues to fascinate many
men and women with her quality designer
clothing, selection, and outstanding service.

ENDA B
MEN & WOMEN

Fashion

4346 W 10th Ave, Vancouver
604.228.1214
enda-b.com

Q and A

What are the most popular or best selling products or services?
Our oldest aroma, Rejuvenating.
Available in lotions, soaps, scrubs and candles. Reed Diffusers and refills.

How do you spend your free time?
With my three children and husband, friends, and family.
Skiing, biking, and dining out.

What was the motivation behind starting your business?
Loved retail and all things that smell great!

What mistake have you made in your business that you will not repeat?
Growing without proper systems in place.

Who is your role model or mentor?
Anita Roddick, founder of The Body Shop.

Jacqui MacNeill

Unique. Sophisticated. Fun.
Escents Aromatherapy's specialty is natural aromatherapy, mood-inspired bath, body, and home fragrancing products. With over 350 different items, each is an adventure for the senses. Take your mind off your worries, unwind, get energized or find balance. It is up to you! Define your mood at Escents as their sophisticated aromas lift and refresh any moment. Escents has grown to eight locations in BC, 24 in Taiwan and now can be found at other premium retail outlets across Canada and the USA.

ESCENTS
AROMATHERAPY

Pamper

1744 Commercial Dr, Vancouver
604.255.4505
escentsaromatherapy.com

EVELINECHARLES
SALONS & SPAS

Pamper, Salon

1495 W 11th, Vancouver
604.678.5666
evelinecharles.com

86

Fashion-Forward. Innovative. Results-Driven. EvelineCharles Salons & Spas is known for its modern, intelligent approach to beauty. Beyond a place for feeling beautiful and head-to-toe pampering, EvelineCharles beauty experts will develop a customized beauty plan for you. Services range from haircuts and colouring to perfect manicures, pedicures, facials and more! You will be educated on the latest trends, personal style and homecare.

Q and A

What was the inspiration behind starting your business?
I have aspired to be an entrepreneur since I was 12 years old. In the small town where I grew up, my aunt owned three different businesses. She was a continuous source of inspiration.

How do you spend your free time?
Scrambling to the top of mountain peaks, running, cooking, entertaining and spending time with my family.

Who is your role model or mentor?
All successful entrepreneurs act as mentors. I am a passionate learner, and a knowledge seeker, therefore as my business changes, I draw on new sources for inspiration to move forward.

What is your indulgence?
Running and food. My greatest indulgence is shopping - I love clothes.

Eveline Charles

87

Where is your favourite place to go with your girlfriends?

I enjoy stealing a friend
or two out to a great
live show, where we can
hear good music, boogie
down, and shake out
all of our cobwebs.

Lisa Osei, Honey Love Design Boutique

88

Exhale Studio
Favourite Gifts
Fine Finds
The Finer Details
Five Corners Media
Flaming Angels Boutique
Forum for Women
  Entrepreneurs (BC)
Front & Company
Gaya
Gloss Salon
Heather Ross [in house]
Hip Baby
Honey Love Design Boutique

EXHALE STUDIO

Fitness

1083 Cambie St., Vancouver (entrance in alley, on 2nd floor)
604.689.2446
exhalestudio.com

Enhances Your Life!

Exhale Studio offers yoga, pilates, AND dance drop-in classes for adults. Each instructor is highly experienced, knowledgeable, and inspiring. Exhale creates a friendly, non-intimidating environment. Located in Vancouver's Yaletown neighbourhood, the studio features warm and exotic coloured walls, beautiful wood floors, and mirrors to reflect the floor-to-ceiling windows facing the tree-lined alley. It's like a Zen tree house!

Q and A

What mistake have you made in your business that you will not repeat?
Trying to do everything myself, not knowing when to delegate, not investing energy in what is most important for the business and me.

How do you spend your free time?
Dancing, pilates, yoga, snowboarding, wake surfing, scuba diving, playing soccer, and travelling.

What was the inspiration behind starting your business?
I love yoga, pilates, and dance. They make the quality of my life better. I wanted to share my passion with like-minded instructors, and together spread the joy to as many people as we can.

What is your indulgence?
Chocolate. Mmmm...

Rachel Wainwright

exhale
YOGA PILATES DANCE STUDIO

Q and A

People may be surprised to know...
I'm actually a homebody, and most
of my socialising is done at the store.

Who is your role model or mentor?
I admire anyone who follows
their dreams and their passion.
It takes a lot of courage to go
against the grain, and I am lucky
to encounter many like-minded
people on a regular basis.

What mistake have you made in your
business that you will not repeat?
Trying to do everything myself.
I've learned to let go of some of
the tasks that I don't enjoy or am
not very good at. I can still be in
control of my finances even if I
don't do my own accounting.

How do you spend your free time?
Hitting the trails for a long run or
curling up with a good book.

Carol Hyslop

Fun. Funky. Fabulous!
Favourite Gifts is a gift and accessory boutique
located in the Lonsdale Quay Market in
beautiful North Vancouver. Showcasing the
latest urban trends, owner Carol Hyslop
brings together independent local artists and
designers under one roof, providing customers
with one or few-of-a-kind goodies. A gift from
Favourite Gifts is sure to become a favourite!

FAVOURITE GIFTS

Lifestyle, Fashion

#219-123 Carrie Cates Ct, North Vancouver
604.904.8840
favouritegifts.ca

FINE FINDS

Fashion

1014 Mainland St, Vancouver
604.669.8325
finefindsboutique.com

Busy. Fun. Challenging.

Fine Finds, located in the heart of Yaletown, is the perfect spot to find a much-needed gift, or the fabulous outfit your closet is missing. This boutique offers an unbelievable selection of clothing, handbags, and jewellery that will leave you feeling complete. Their customers claim Find Finds to be their favourite store in the city!

Q and A

Jane McFadden and Megan Maxwell (not pictured)

What are the most popular or best selling products or services?
Our customers come in often to purchase the perfect gift, and leave with a new outfit, complete with shoes, a handbag, a killer necklace, and a new onesie for the baby shower they're attending.

People may be surprised to know...
That we've been open for eight years, and we opened as a furniture store.

Who is your role model or mentor?
My husband awakes at 5am every morning, and insists on making his business better everyday. That inspires me to work harder.

What was the inspiration behind starting your business?
My grandfather owned stores and both my parents have been entrepreneurs for much of their lives as is my brother. I guess it's in my blood.

95

Q and A

What are the most popular or best selling products or services?
Corporate wine and cheese receptions, appreciation events, and holiday parties.

What mistake have you made in your business that you will not repeat?
Following my heart more than my head. It is hard to realise that being a business owner means making tough decisions that as an individual I might not make.

What was the motivation behind starting your business?
My desire to be the boss, provide an excellent level of customer service, and connect with businesses on a personal level.

People may be surprised to know...
I used to train Fitness Leaders for the YMCA.

Deborah Wallace

Efficient. Caring. Creative.
Deborah Wallace brings a bright smile and pizazz to the organization of corporate events in Vancouver. With a flair for setting realistic goals, selecting unique vendors, and creating a memorable party theme, her events are guaranteed to reflect polish and entertain guests. The Finer Details team will tend to all the finer details, so everyone can relax and enjoy!

THE FINER DETAILS

Event Services

604.689.1463
thefinerdetails.ca

FIVE CORNERS MEDIA presents

WWW.FIVE-CORNERS.CA

bringing you fashion, food, drink, play
& the quality of life to fully engage
yourself in Vancouver

Melissa Joaquin

Q and A

What are the most popular or best selling products or services?
Our newsletters offer exclusive info, updates, and prizes, plus our networking events create a non-intimidating platform to capture creativity.

People may be surprised to know...
I also run a vitamin manufacturing company, called Nutramedics, with my brothers.

What was the inspiration behind starting your business?
Coming out of college, I felt very fortunate to have a family business, and support. Many young professionals have amazing ideas, but need the resources and connections to harvest them. That is where Five Corners comes in.

What is your indulgence?
Shoes! Particularly Jimmy Choo and Christian Louboutin.

Sassy. Stylish. Approachable.
Five Corners Media is a young professional's lifestyle guide to the city. Owner Melissa Joaquin gives you the heads up of where to spend your hard-earned cash, and where to go on your well-deserved time off. Whether you want to relax, network, or party, Five Corners Media will be your guide. Their website offers daily features, weekly newsletters, feature articles by local writers, networking events, and business-development workshops.

MELISSA JOAQUIN
FOUNDER & EDITOR
WWW.FIVE-CORNERS.CA
T 604 688 7854
E MELISSA@FIVE-CORNERS.CA

FIVE CORNERS MEDIA

Media

five-corners.ca

Q and A

What are the most popular or best selling products or services?
Our funky, novelty-print pillows; sushi; and skull and rose tattoos.

People may be surprised to know...
That our shop features mostly local designers and jewellers.

What was the motivation behind starting your business?
I wanted to show Vancouver that dark and edgy can be fun and light-hearted too.

Who is your role model or mentor?
I enjoying bouncing ideas off friends and family. My staff are very helpful and honest too.

How do you spend your free time?
Going to the movies, out dancing with friends, checking out art shows.

Miriam Melanson

Edgy. Original. Fun.
Flaming Angels is a steadily-growing boutique, interested in every facet of dark and avant-garde fashion and home decor. Owner Miriam Melanson's mission is to provide arresting, distinctive, and sinfully enticing apparel and accessories for the darker cravings of Vancouver and elsewhere.

FLAMING ANGELS
BOUTIQUE

Fashion

644 Seymour St, Vancouver
604.689.3224
flamingangels.net

FORUM FOR WOMEN ENTREPRENEURS (BC)

Networking

604.682.8115
fwe.ca

Mentoring. Educating. Networking.
The Forum for Women Entrepreneurs (FWE) is an organization for women building and leading high-growth companies. Its mission is to mentor and educate women entrepreneurs through five core programs: e-series program, a-series program, student internship program, roundtable events, and the mentor program. FWE BC is a registered non-profit society in the province of BC, with over 500 active members.

People may be surprised to know...
Although our programs are designed to support female entrepreneurs, we have both men and women actively engaged in our organization as speakers, mentors, and supporters.

What was the motivation behind starting your business?
A need in this market to mentor and educate women entrepreneurs, with high growth business models.

Who is your role model or mentor?
We are inspired by the passion and determination of all women entrepreneurs.

Where is your favourite place to go with your girlfriends?
FWE events including roundtable events, the e-series graduation event, and especially the annual Gala Celebration.

Christina Anthony,
Founder Chair and President

Jill Earthy
Executive Director

103

FRONT & COMPANY

Lifestyle

3772 Main St, Vancouver
604.879.8431
frontandcompany.ca

Ever-Evolving. Refreshing.
Supported by 5000+ consignors and loyal customers, Front and Company survived from a recent fire and reopened in Fall 2008 with bigger dreams. With twice as much retail space, Front is ready to embark her new journey of sharing beauty and style in consignment, as well as new clothing. Along with endless lines of elegant and fun accessories and giftware, Front continues to provide an inspiring place for the enjoyment of shopping.

 Q and A

What are the most popular or best selling products or services?
Quality, trendsetting, consigned fashion. Fun and personal gifts. Jewellery and accessories.

People may be surprised to know...
It is Front's 15th birthday this year!

What was the motivation behind starting your business?
The quest for treasure hunting, especially in hope of people showing up with great finds and one-of-a-kind vintage pieces at our consignment counter.

Who is your role model or mentor?
Diana: Guido in the movie
8-1/2 by Fellini.
Flora: Diana!

Diana Li &
Flora Cheung

Q and A

People may be surprised to know...
Gaya is run by 3 sisters who
are in charge of design,
production, and marketing.

Who is your role model or mentor?
Our father, who has been in the
shoe business for over 30 years.

What mistake have you made in your
business that you will not repeat?
Functionality of the handbag
is as important as the style.

How do you spend your free time?
Spending time with family
and our beloved dog, Kiki.

What was the inspiration behind
starting your business?
The in house designer, Wei
Wei Chang, believes that what
you carry on your arm tells so
much about who you are.

Stylish. Unique. Fun.
From Vancouver, to North America, to Europe
and Asia, Gaya has been gaining recognition
in the fashion world. Defined by eclectic
designs and a trademark peony logo, the
company is now going into its sixth year
of crafting quality, stylish handbags and
accessories that fashion lovers everywhere
look for. Gaya collections have been
featured in fashion magazines worldwide.

Sally, Wei Wei,
and Angela Chang

GAYA CANADA ENTERPRISES

Fashion

#232-1868 Glen Dr, Vancouver
604.738.0977
gaya.ca

GLOSS SALON

Salon

3149 Granville St, Vancouver
604.732.8282
glosshair.biz

People may be surprised to know...
I have a restaurant named
after me (Chow).

How do you spend your free time?
Planning events and trying
to get organised.

Who is your role model or mentor?
My sister.

What was the inspiration behind
starting your business?
To create a space to share with
the people I work with, for us
to enjoy and have fun in.

Where is the best place
to buy clothes?
Moulé. They have everything,
including great clothes for
men, women, and kids.

What is your indulgence?
Dinner with friends.

Contemporary. Fun. Chic.
Gloss up your life! This unique salon on
South Granville boasts two floors of eclectic
artistry. Colour, texture, fashion, fun -- toes
and nails to come. Visit Gloss for fresh takes
on contemporary style without pretence or
overblown expense. These award-winning
stylists know how to do it all, from classic to
edgy, with unwavering attention to detail
and commitment to you and your fab self.

Ceanne
Chow

HEATHER ROSS
[in house]

Lifestyle

1525 W 6th Ave, Vancouver
604.738.4284
heatherrossinhouse.com

Evocative. Eclectic. Original.

Heather Ross offers an eclectic mix of art and home decor. Recently expanded into a more spacious, elemental gallery/boutique, Heather's alluring paintings and photographs mix artfully amongst treasures both new and old, gathered from her world travels. Heather's wonderful sense of colour, keen eye for design, and love of nature can be seen in charming displays and vignettes. Pure, simple ceramics and modern fresh accessories mingle amongst the layers and patinas of textiles, antiques, and natural objects, creating an atmosphere that is tactile, serene, and inviting.

Q and A

What are the most popular or best selling products or services?
My paintings, quirky one-of-a-kind finds, and little simple pleasures like pure soy candles.

What was the inspiration behind starting your business?
As a young artisan I could not find anyone I wanted to work for, so I just began making things for my own company.

What mistake have you made in your business that you will not repeat?
Early on, I did not factor in the physical limitations to doing and making everything myself.

Where is your favourite place to go with your girlfriends?
I love to catch up with my friends on a patio on a rare sunny eve, or go for a healthy walk along the beach together.

Heather Ross

HIPBABY

Children's

2110 W 4th Ave, Vancouver
604.737.0603
hipbaby.com

Baby and Parenting Supplies.
Hipbaby is Vancouver's coolest baby store, offering must-have products for the urban parent. Having been around for 11 years, it's no secret that owner Carla van Messel has stocked her store with a great selection of basics, and exceptional, specialty items, all priced affordably. Her beginnings include the denial of pink and blue baby traditions, in favour of black and white.

Carla
van Messel

 Q and A

People may be surprised to know...
We design and manufacture 40% of what we sell. 25% of our inventory does not repeat, so there are new things all the time.

What mistake have you made in your business that you will not repeat?
Trying to expand the store's zone concept.

How do you spend your free time?
With my family - five kids, three dogs and two cats. Biking, snowboarding, swimming, cooking.

What is your indulgence?
Dark chocolate and 50 days of snowboarding a year.

What are the most popular or best selling products or services?
Baby tees, cloth diapers, and diaper bags.

113

Q and A

What was the motivation behind starting your business?
I became tired of working hard for others and not feeling appreciated. It was time to put this energy and all of my experience into myself, and to prove to myself what I could do instead of daydreaming about it.

Who is your role model or mentor?
My mother would spend endless hours with me teaching me to sew when I was a little girl. She would design and create such beautiful things for me. I grew up watching and learning. She is a great business woman, and always reminded me that I could do anything I set my mind to! Nothing is impossible.

What is your indulgence?
Shopping for flowers and fine foods. I enjoy cooking and entertaining. Also French lingerie and Aveda Products.

Lisa Osei

Feminine. Unique. Chic.
Bursting with ultra-girly, feminine fashions, Honey Love Design Boutique brings to life the feeling of walking into your dream closet. Let their expert stylists dress you from head to toe. Along with locally-made jewellery, accessories, shoes, gifts, and body-care products designed exclusively for the boutique, you will find the Honey Love Design Label. It's owner Lisa Osei's aspiration to be sure you leave feeling good about yourself!

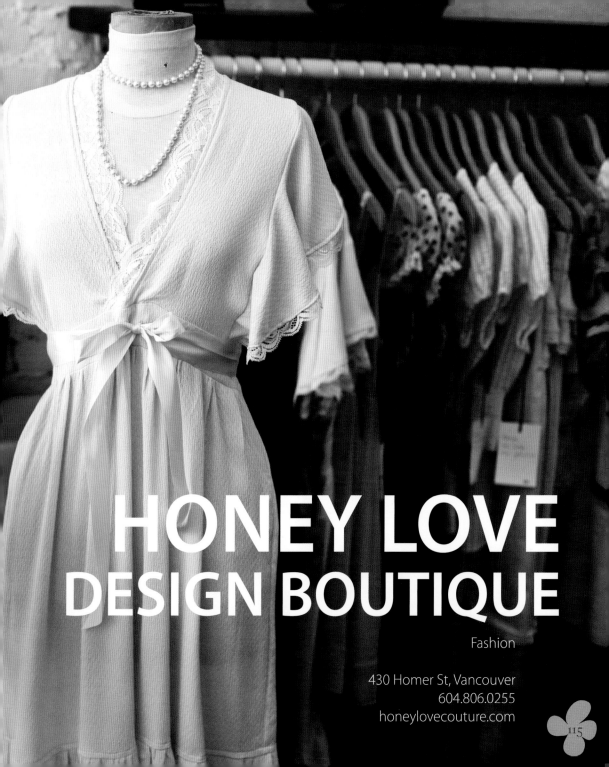

HONEY LOVE
DESIGN BOUTIQUE

Fashion

430 Homer St, Vancouver
604.806.0255
honeylovecouture.com

115

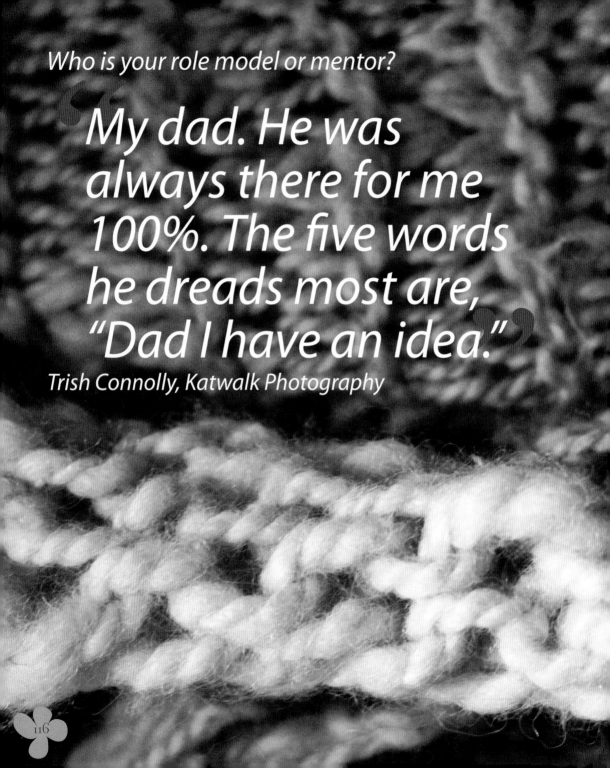

Who is your role model or mentor?

"*My dad. He was always there for me 100%. The five words he dreads most are, "Dad I have an idea.*""

Trish Connolly, Katwalk Photography

Larry Designs

The Honey Mustard
  Fashion & Media Services
  and Fashion High
Höng Photography Studio
Ishara
Jag Dhahan
JC Studio
Jeweliette
Jo's Toes and Esthetics
Kalena's Italian Shoes
  & Accessories
Katwalk Photography
Kim Allan Silk
Larry Designs
Le Petit Spa
Liquid

117

THE HONEY MUSTARD
FASHION & MEDIA SERVICES

FASHION HIGH

Media

604.734.5674
thehoneymustard.com
fashionhigh.ca

Creative. Local. Fashionable.

Sarah Murray is Style Director for The Honey Mustard. While designers create fashion, and boutiques make sales, The Honey Mustard works on all the elements required to make brands recognizable to the media and public. She is also the founder of Fashion High, a not-for-profit association of fashion industry professionals who are working to educate the public about Vancouver's local fashion industry and sustainable design.

 Q and A

What are the most popular or best selling products or services?
Publicity is our bread and butter, but we also do one fashion show a month on average.

What mistake have you made in your business that you will not repeat?
Working without a subcontractor contract, oops.

How do you spend your free time?
Definitely not on the computer, I love to read novels.

What is your indulgence?
Dresses - new and vintage.

Where is the best place to get a pedicure?
Float Relaxation Lounge. I love the atmosphere and the soothing fish tank.

Sarah Murray

Ellen
Ho

 Q and A

What are the most popular or best selling products or services?
Wedding photography and portraits sessions.

People may be surprised to know...
I used to design clothes!

What was the inspiration behind starting your business?
My passion in photography and art.

What mistake have you made in your business that you will not repeat?
Selling myself short.

How do you spend your free time?
With my loved ones and my beloved Boston Terrier.

What is your indulgence?
Watching movies, eating exquisite food.

Chic. Unique. Refreshing.
Höng Wedding Photography Studio is a boutique-style studio for people who are in love! Inspired by your love stories, Ellen Ho passionately strives to capture the most intimate and exquisite moments of your special day. She believes these moments are what make each photo and wedding extraordinary. If you like something chic, something unique, and something elegant, Höng is for you!

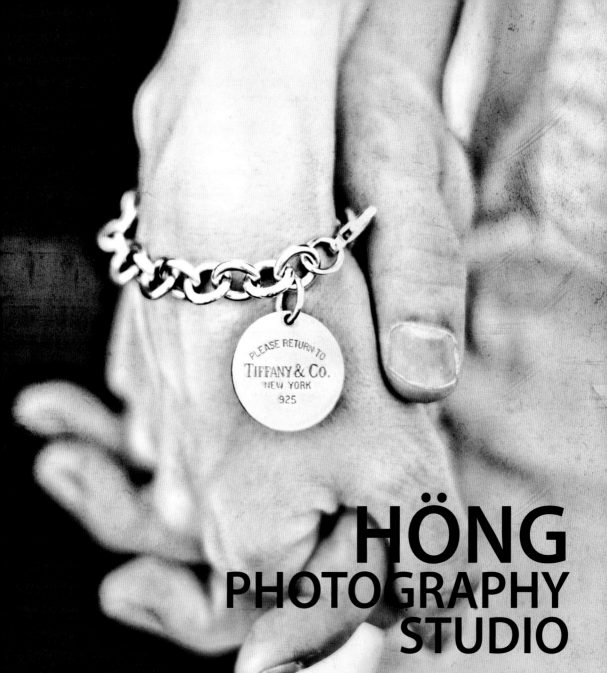

HÖNG
PHOTOGRAPHY STUDIO

Photography

778.228.6256
hong-photography.com

121

Q and A

Who is your role model or mentor?
My husband. He has an affinity
for business and is a strong
entrepreneurial force in my life.

What is your indulgence?
I indulge in indulging -
anything and everything!

Where is your favourite place
to go with your girlfriends?
Anywhere new. Getting dressed up
and going for dinner or cocktails
with girlfriends regularly is a must.

What was the inspiration behind
starting your business?
I wanted to give women in
Vancouver the selection and
comfort I had experienced only
when shopping in other cities
or countries. I wanted to provide
exceptional service and exceptional
products - a place where women
could come to expect the best.

Amrit Baidwan

Luxury. Style.
Ishara is a tightly edited assortment of rare and
exceptional clothing collections inspired by
luxury. The items found in Ishara benefit from
great design and fashion-forward style, without
sacrificing quality. Owner Amrit Baidwan has
brought together some of the best pieces
from noted designers to provide an ultimate
closet where women can shop comfortably,
and choose the perfect outfit knowing
that it won't be found everywhere else.

good clothes open all doors

ISHARA

123

JAG DHAHAN

Pamper

778.772.3301
jagdhahan.com

Creative. Reliable. Versatile.

Since attending Blanche MacDonald almost three years ago, Jag Dhahan has been a freelance makeup artist in the Lower Mainland. She offers mobile makeup services for special occasions, bridal, graduations, photo shoots, and fashion shows, including both airbrush tanning and makeup. She also provides makeup application lessons. Jag loves working with different ethnicities and complexions. She can produce a very wide range of looks, from everyday, to fantasy makeup!

 Q and A

What are the most popular or best selling products or services?
Makeup application for special occasions such as weddings, graduations or a night on the town!

Who is your role model or mentor?
I really respect and admire the work of Charlie Green. She's best known for working with Victoria's Secret's legendary runway shows.

How do you spend your free time?
I love to watch The Food Network and try out new restaurants and recipes. Cooking is my other passion.

Where is your favourite place to go with your girlfriends?
Out for dinner at one of Vancouver's many fresh seafood restaurants, especially where there's a nice view!

What is your indulgence?
Cosmetics. I never leave a store empty-handed.

Jag Dhahan

JC STUDIO

Fashion

46 W 6th Ave, Vancouver
604.688.5222
jcstudio.ca

126

Modern Shopping Experience.

JC Studio is the home of the Jacqueline Conoir Collection, and Vancouver's most modern shopping experience. Designer RozeMerie Cuevas embodies current trends without compromising the modern, yet timeless, elegance of fashion today. It is RozeMerie's absolute pleasure to combine creative looks that bring out your unique and individual personality. Once you wear Jacqueline Conoir, you will be noticed!

RozeMerie Cuevas

Q and A

What are the most popular or best selling products or services?
Our "Fashionista Brunch" books up quickly. On Saturdays at 10:30am and 1:00pm, enjoy mimosas, a light brunch, a mini fashion show, a fashion seminar, and shopping like a star.

People may be surprised to know...
We are not just a suiting collection. We have the perfect modern outfit, for everything from work to casual, and from clubbing to formal.

What mistake have you made in your business that you will not repeat?
Being too afraid to take chances.

How do you spend your free time?
With my teenagers, eating at Chambar, cooking, entertaining, skiing, and snowboarding.

JEWELIETTE

Jewellery

692 Seymour St, Vancouver
604.687.5577
jeweliette.com

Q and A

Beautiful. Sparkly. Unique.
Playground to Vancouver's premier costume designers, stylists, and social set, Jeweliette has been offering their tempting array of accessories and jewellery to the city's most glamourous personalities for close to two decades. Run by Madalena Corsi and her jewellery-designer daughter, Elsa Corsi, the salon style atmosphere shared with couturier Manuel Mendoza offers everything from classic pearls, to red-carpet-worthy rhinestones.

People may be surprised to know...
That we work and live together, and still actually get along.

Where is the best place to buy shoes?
Italy!

What was the inspiration behind starting your business?
If you have to spend most of your life working, then it might as well be somewhere you love to go. A place where you are surrounded by beautiful objects and creative people.

Where is the best place to buy clothes?
Vetrina Moda.

Who is the best local designer?
Manuel Mendoza.

What is the best gym or fitness club?
The walk to work every day!

Madalena and Elsa Corsi

Jeweliette
Jewellery ♛ Accessories

What are the most popular or best selling products or services?
My best selling service is definitely the nail art. I get clients of all ages, from age three to 80, and from all over the Lower Mainland and other countries. My favourite and best selling facial treatment is Botinol, which has a Botox-like effect, but without injections. It repairs inner-layer skin damage, intensely hydrates, and prevents further damage.

People may be surprised to know...
I was a tomboy growing up, and never knew how to take care of myself!

How do you spend your free time?
I enjoy being outdoors as much as possible, and am a very active person. I walk, hike, swim, dance, cook, socialise with friends, paint, and I also DJ now and then.

Joanna Konkin

Fun. Peaceful. Satisfying.
Joanna Konkin has enjoyed the esthetics field for eight years and is thrilled to be running her own business, Jo's Toes, for the past six. She provides full esthetics services to both men and women, including manicures, pedicures, waxing, threading, eye lash tinting, reiki, reflexology, and a series of different anti-aging facial treatments, using GM Collin products. Her specialty is doing hand-painted, custom-designed nail art on toenails.

JO'S TOES & ESTHETICS

Pamper

#212-2233 Burrard St, Vancouver
604.736.1200
jostoes.com

KALENA'S ITALIAN SHOES AND ACCESSORIES

Shoes

1526 Commercial Dr, Vancouver
604.255.3727
kalenashoes.com

Ultimate. Specialty. Italian.

Kalena's was founded by a young Italian named Carmine, and his new bride Isa. The newlyweds headed to Italy in the summer of 1967 on their first buying trip, which also doubled as their Honeymoon. Their goal was to provide fashion-forward, high-quality, Italian footwear at reasonable prices. Over the years, Kalena's has had several secondary locations throughout Vancouver, but the Commercial Drive store located in the heart of Little Italy, has always been considered home.

Veralena and
Isa D'Onofrio

Q and A

People may be surprised to know...
That we have been in business for over 41 years. We travel to Italy on biannual buying trips, and purchase our shoes and handbags directly from the manufacturers.

How do you spend your free time?
Skiing, skating, spending time with family and friends.

What was the inspiration behind starting your business?
The belief in providing beautiful, high-quality products that we take pride in offering to our customers.

Where is your favourite place to go with your girlfriends?
Out for dinner to a nice restaurant like Joe Fortes or Vij's so we can chat without day-to-day interruptions, while enjoying a lovely glass of Prosecco.

Q and A

What mistake have you made in your business that you will not repeat?
I learned early on that overhead can be a monster.

Who is the best local designer?
I fell in love with Simply Sublime while photographing the store for this book. They have AMAZING things!

People may be surprised to know...
How shy I really am.

What was the motivation behind starting your business?
Turning a passion into my full-time business.

Where is your favourite place to go with your girlfriends?
The Keg for Crab Dip and Strawberry Daquries at midnight.

Trish Connolly

Affordable. Fun. Professional.
Katwalk Photography is a one-stop shop for photography services. Owner Trish Connolly offers everything from fashion, commercial, and product shots, to headshots, portfolio work, and makeovers. Katwalk's studios offer large ready rooms with makeup and hair stations, wardrobe and accessories, wind machines, and more. Services include digital touchups and enhancements, file sizing, and file archiving for six months. Katwalk also specializes in working with all budget sizes, and they know you will be pleasantly surprised at how affordable professional images can be.

KATWALK PHOTOGRAPHY

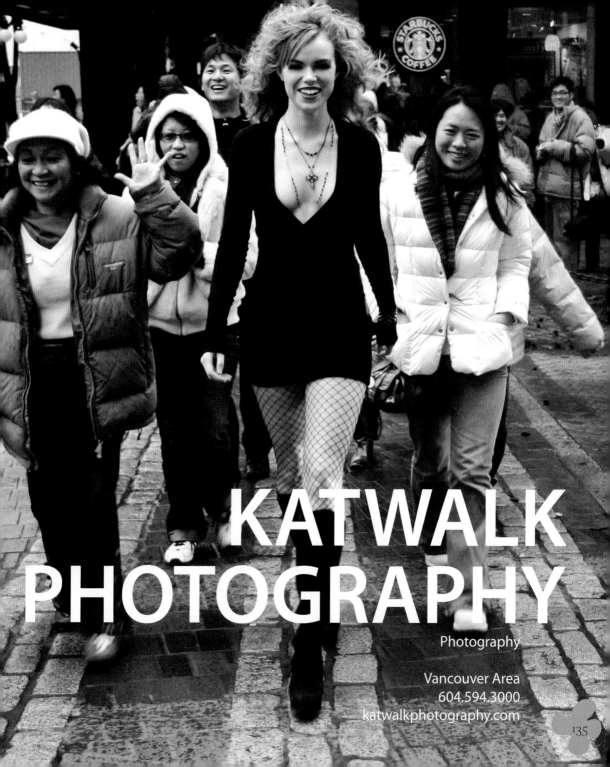

KATWALK
PHOTOGRAPHY

Photography

Vancouver Area
604.594.3000
katwalkphotography.com

135

KIM ALLAN SILK

Fashion

604.922.5366
kimallansilk.com

Dynamic. Growing. Fun.
Kim Allan Silk sells luxurious silk knit garments that are meant to be worn everyday. You won't find lace, or fancy fads here. Kim Allan Silk produces ultra-comfortable, sensible silk garments that are explicitly designed to make people of all sizes and ages feel good. They are travellers' favourites due to easy packing and care. There are over 140 stores in Canada that offer Kim Allan Silk, and web customers all over the world!

Kim Allan

Q and A

What are the most popular or best selling products or services?
People are addicted to the underwear. Comfortable, sexy, yet sensible. Matching camisoles are also very popular.

What was the motivation behind starting your business?
Being my own boss!

People may be surprised to know...
That many celebrities wear KAS Long Johns under their clothes on cold movie shoots.

How do you spend your free time?
Hiking up Capilano Canyon and training for marathons.

What is your indulgence?
White wine and french fries!

Where is your favourite place to go with your girlfriends?
Fishing trips and Las Vegas.

137

LARRY DESIGNS

Fashion

604.644.7612
wearelarry.com

138

Unique. Warm. Minimalist.

Larry Designs is a striking, minimalist knitwear accessories line produced in Vancouver, BC. Local alpaca fiber is processed naturally and spun by hand into lush oversized yarn, which designer Terri Potratz uses to construct unique pieces, such as long, bulky scarves, and cozy, buttoned neck warmers.

 Q and A

Terri Potratz

People may be surprised to know...
I buy my alpaca fiber direct from the farmer who raises them, have the fleece processed naturally and hand spun at a co-op mill in BC, and hand knit all pieces myself. The foundation of Larry Designs was built upon a desire to work with local resources and businesses.

What was the motivation behind starting your business?
I wanted a very large, long scarf last winter and couldn't find one anywhere. My only option was to learn how to knit one myself, and once I completed it I had so many compliments and requests that starting a business was a no-brainer.

Who is your role model or mentor?
My mom. Without her and her knitting circle as my expert resources, I'm not sure how far I would have gotten on that original scarf!

Q and A

What are the most popular or best selling products or services?
Signature facials, Brazilian waxing, Phytomer skin care, Jane Iredale pressed minerals.

People may be surprised to know...
I can't sit down for very long.

What was the motivation behind starting your business?
To be my own boss and still be as creative as possible.

What mistake have you made in your business that you will not repeat?
Poor financing.

How do you spend your free time?
Golf, walking, drinking wine.

What is your indulgence?
Sauvignon Blanc.

Nancy Mudford

Beautiful. Serene. Tranquil.
Le Petit Spa represents the embodiment of a lifelong dream for owner, Nancy Mudford. She's proud of her achievements in creating a beautiful and inviting space, and delivering exceptional professional spa services, which include facials, waxing, massage, pedicures, manicures, and make-up application. Gift certificates are available online or at the spa.

LE PETIT SPA

Pamper

3701 W Broadway, Vancouver
604.224.4314
lepetitspa.ca

Krista
Mennell

Q and A

People may be surprised to know...
We've moved to Main Street
from 4th Avenue!

Who is your role model or mentor?
I never thought I would do what I do
without my step father's guidance.

What is your indulgence?
Sweets.

How do you spend your free time?
Hanging out with friends
and my dog, riding my bike,
design blogs, meditation

What was the inspiration
or motivation behind
starting your business?
I wanted to work for myself.

Where is your favourite place
to go with your girlfriends?
For dessert!

Bigger. Brighter. Better.
Destination Liquid. Nestled on funky Main
Street, Liquid makes a splash with eclectic
clothing and jewellery collections, from
modern coquettish to playful pretty. If you
love local and international lines, you'll love
Liquid. For over eight years, this fresh mecca
has been serving up such infamous Canadian
designers as Allison Wonderland, Adesif,
and Eve Gravel, just to name a few. Liquid is
uncommon fashion for the singular woman.

LIQUID
CLOTHING

LIQUID

Fashion

2337 Main St, Vancouver
604.569.2468

143

People may be surprised to know...

"*Our first business was selling tie-dyed scrunchies when we were in grade 3!*"

Genevieve Ennis and Zoe Pawlak, Loaded Bow

Lolo Jewellery

Little Nest
Loaded Bow
Lola Home & Apparel
Lolo Jewellery
M0851
Make It Productions/Bootyfly
 Bags/No BS Headband
Malary's Fashion Network
Mally Bibs
Mango Design Co.
Marimekko Vancouver
Markus J Hair & Well-Being
Masik
Maude Salon

LITTLE NEST

Eats

1716 Charles Street, East Vancouver
604.251.9994
littlenest.ca

146

Communal. Nurturing. Warm.

Little Nest is a haven for families and foodies alike. This "parent-friendly" neighbourhood café, located just off Vancouver's Commercial Drive, earned itself critical acclaim (and a loyal following) within weeks of opening. The kitchen's menu is constantly evolving, with thought and care always given to the seasonality, locality, freshness and integrity of ingredients. The café's large open space is whimsical, airy and light, a place where kids are free to be kids, while grown ups can still feel grown up.

 Q and A

What are the most popular or best selling products or services?
The eggs of the day: organic, free-range eggs, toasted organic baguette, and whatever takes our fancy that morning. The same goes for the muffins that change daily, depending on what's in season.

What mistake have you made in your business that you will not repeat?
Paying too much attention to the small amount of negative criticism, and not enough to the great deal of positive. You lose your direction when you try to please everyone, and you get nowhere when you try to please those that are never happy.

Who is your role model or mentor?
Alice Waters of Chez Panisse, and more recently as a defender of Slow Food and Founder of the Edible Schoolyard Project. I don't know her personally, but admire her greatly and I find her story so inspiring.

Mary Macintyre

 Q and A

What are the most popular or best selling products or services?
Interviews with fabulous women, such as the Smart Cookies and Donna Fenn.

What mistake have you made in your business that you will not repeat?
Straying from our mission.

What was the motivation behind starting your business?
We were amazed at how a blog posting about Zoe's paintings fuelled her sales – we had to get online!

Who is your role model or mentor?
We are inspired by ALL women who forge their own paths and create sustainable, viable businesses for themselves and their families.

Where is your favourite place to go with your girlfriends?
We love to go out for meals, Vancouver is an amazing place to eat!

Informative. Passionate. Inspiring.
Loaded Bow is a blog that was founded by two friends who have a deep respect for the pure passion that drives all entrepreneurs. The blog seeks to explore the experiences and accomplishments of the female business founder, and to facilitate her growth through information, resources and stories, so that she may approach her business with confidence and conviction.

Genevieve Ennis and Zoe Pawlak

LOADED BOW

Networking

loadedbow.com

LOLA HOME & APPAREL

Children's, Fashion, Lifestyle

1076 Hamilton St, Vancouver
604.633.5017
lolahomeandapparel.com

150

Chic. Eccentric. Quirky.

Think French-whimsy meets English-eccentricity, with a New-York twist. An unusual blend of girly-boudoir-meets-edgy-fashionista. Lola mixes and matches vintage tea sets, crystal chandeliers, and Diptyque candles, with Tocca slip dresses, quirky separates, denim, and designer handbags, as well as Burberry Baby, Petit Bateau, and heirloom silver, making it the city's most chic one-stop shop.

Q and A

What was the inspiration behind starting your business?
I was inspired by the familiar charm of Paris and London neighbourhood boutique shopping.

What mistake have you made in your business that you will not repeat?
Assuming that staff would be able to express my enthusiasm as passionately as I do. This is not possible. I am, and always will be, my best employee because the shop is my vision.

What is your indulgence?
Escaping to the Gulf Islands for a few days, where time seems to stand still.

What advice would you give to women starting their own business?
Start small, be flexible, and always remember that there is a solution to everything.

Christina McDaniel

151

Q and A

People may be surprised to know...
I started my first business at
the age of eight, selling home-
baked cookies to classrooms
at my elementary school.

What was the inspiration behind
starting your business?
I have always wanted to create
my own brand by designing a
fashion related product. Having
your own business gives you
flexibility and freedom... something
you need when you're a mom.

Who is your role model or mentor?
My 2 year old daughter Stella
is my mentor. She shows me
daily that it's the simple things
in life that make us happy.

What is your indulgence?
Late-night cooking and baking.

Lorena Ponis

Classic. Timeless. Versatile.
Lolo Jewellery & Accessories is a quality line
of high-end fashion jewellery, and leather
handbags. Their collections are classic, timeless,
and versatile, catering to every woman. Lolo is
available in various high-end boutiques across
Canada, online, and soon in the UK and USA.

152

LOLO JEWELLERY
& ACCESSORIES

Jewellery

604.937.8508
lolo.ca

153

Kimberly
Pao

Q and A

What was the motivation behind starting your business?
I loved the company and products so much that after six years with the corporate office, I had an opportunity to branch out on my own and bring m0851 to the West Coast.

People may be surprised to know...
That I was an English major and technical writer before working in retail sales.

Who is your role model or mentor?
My sister. She has lived in five different countries, and is now a partner at Deloitte and Touche Shanghai. She taught me to take risks, and that hard work really pays off.

What is your indulgence?
Designer shoes, Christian Louboutins in particular.

Timeless. Classic. Minimal.
M0851, formerly Rugby North America, is a Montreal-based design house that specializes in leather bags and accessories, alongside clothing and raincoats. Their emphasis is on creating styles that are clean and timeless, while focusing on the product rather than the brand. M0851 handcrafts all their products in Montreal, and has stores now in Montreal, Toronto, New York, Vancouver, Taipei, Paris, and Antwerp.

M0851

Fashion

1035 Alberni St, Vancouver
604.688.9575
m0851.com

155

MAKE IT PRODUCTIONS
BOOTYFLY BAGS
NO BS HEADBAND

Event Services, Fashion

778.233.7468
makeitproductions.com
bootyflybags.com
nobsheadband.com

Inspired. Energetic. Effervescent.
Make It is a retail show devoted to creating positive and lucrative opportunities for artists, crafters, and designers. On the flip side, Make It is a shopping event that gives enlightened shoppers the opportunity to buy unique, ethically-made goods from top Canadian artisans. The vibe at the show is funky, hip and modern; very different from your traditional granny craft show! The next event is May 2-3 2009 at the Roundhouse in Yaletown.

 Q and A

Jenna
Herbut

What are the most popular or best selling products or services?
My Bootyfly Bags have been selling extremely well at retail shows all over the country. They are reversible and come with two interchangeable straps. The No Bunch or Slide (BS) Headband is also a huge hit because it does in fact live up to its lofty title!

What was the inspiration behind starting your business?
I had little businesses since I was a child. In junior high, my mom would pick me up after school so I could go on "sales calls."

Who is your role model or mentor?
I really admire any women who combines business with a sense of fun and passion for life. I think Betsey Johnson is the epitome of this.

What is your indulgence?
I love a good boot! I probably have 30 pairs.

Q and A

Who is your role model or mentor?
Barbara Walters or any other woman that has pursued their passion and persevered against many odds and adversities to accomplish what they strived for.

What are the most popular or best selling products or services?
TAB (The Amazing Bra) custom-fitted bras and undergarments, evening gowns, and special occasion dresses and suits.

How do you spend your free time?
I bicycle, play piano, read biographies of inspirational people, and enjoy a relaxing dinner or lunch with good friends.

What is your indulgence?
Massages, pedicures, hair styles, manicures... anything spa!

Yvonne Hogenes

Unique. Exciting. Cutting-Edge.

Malary's Fashion Network is a boutique located in downtown Cloverdale, and has celebrated 10 successful years of offering clients the ultimate shopping experience. Malary's is known for its comprehensive selection of evening wear and gowns, and accessories to match. Many of the selections are one-of-a-kind dresses by Vancouver designers. To help make these garments fit perfectly, Malary's has designed and manufactured the TAB (The Amazing Bra) custom-fitted bras. These bras have no underwires, no elastic, and are offered in 125 sizes!

158

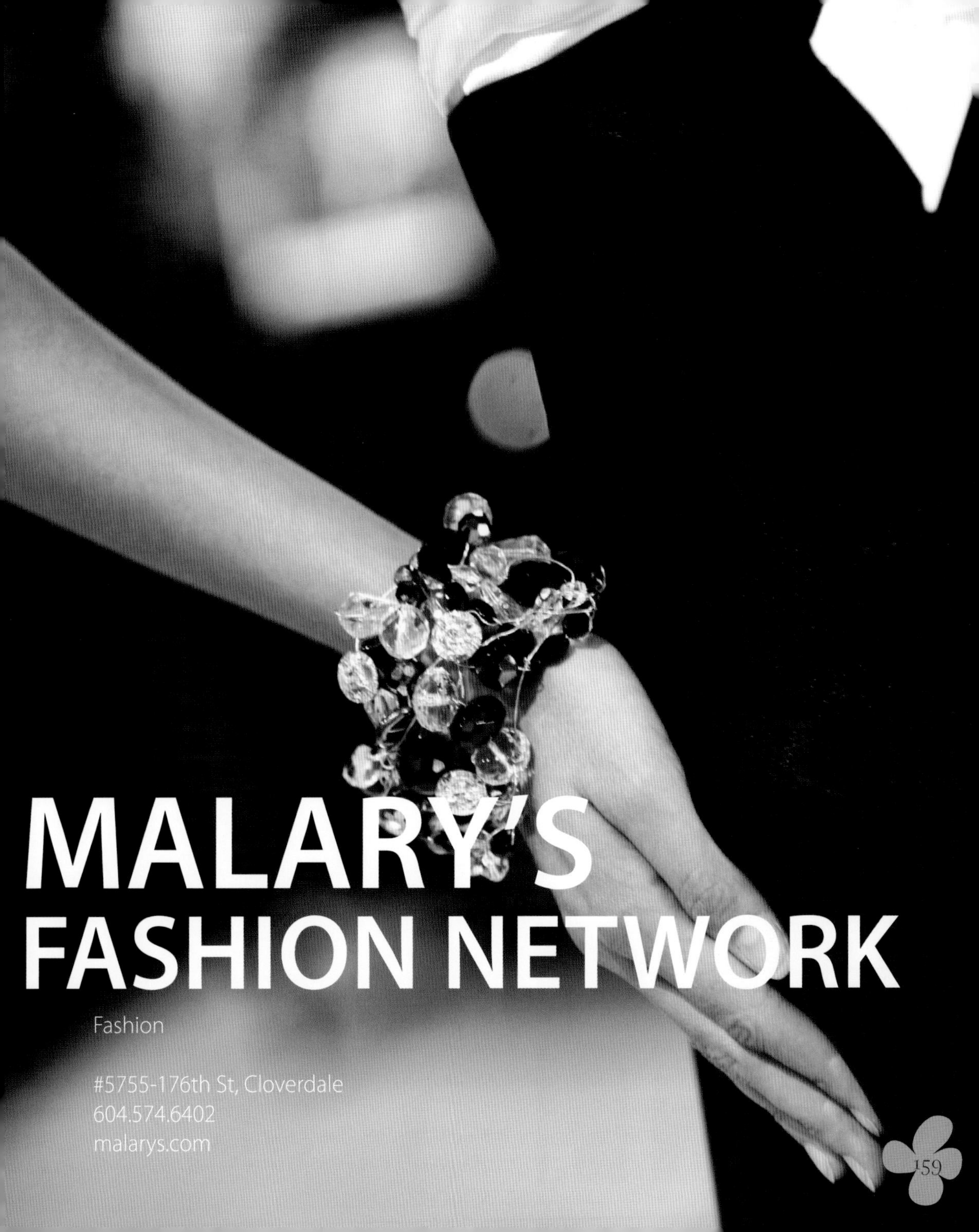

MALARY'S
FASHION NETWORK

Fashion

#5755-176th St, Cloverdale
604.574.6402
malarys.com

159

What are the most popular or best selling products or services?
The most popular designs overall are monkey, bee, and caterpillar. The most popular online option is customized bibs.

What was the inspiration behind starting your business?
My children. My daughter Malia, at 10 months old, was the inspiration for the idea of a leather baby bib. After laundering dozens of cloth bibs per week, I was determined to design something better!

What mistake have you made in your business that you will not repeat?
Lack of research. When tackling new challenges such as exporting or distributing, research is key.

What is your indulgence?
Coconut Cream Pie - mmmmmmm!

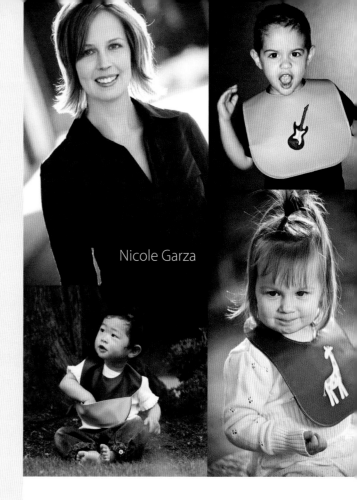

Nicole Garza

Exciting. Fulfilling. Inspiring.
Mally Bibs are the original leather baby bib. Leather is durable, easily wipes clean, and is safe and comfortable, making it the perfect material for bibs. Mally Bibs are designed not only for function, but also for style. Each bib includes a child friendly design on one side, and a food-catch pocket option on the other. Available in dozens of designs, they are a must have for any new parent!

MALLY BIBS

Children's

MANGO DESIGN CO

Stylist

#910-207 W Hastings St, Vancouver
604.875.1730
mangodesignco.ca

Modern. Organic. Romantic.
Mango Design Company provides green design for modern dwellings. Owner and creative director Tanya McLean is a LEED® accredited residential designer, with a serious passion for the planet. Mango's organic philosophy translates into a timeless modernism that resonates purity, simplicity, and balance.

What are the most popular or best selling products or services?
Mango has grown over the past five years from simply providing drafting and decor services, to extensive whole home renovations, multi-unit residential interiors, and boutique commercial projects. Where we were initially nudging our clients into "greenness," we are now being sought out to do so!

People may be surprised to know...
I'm happiest with bare feet, a bungalow on the beach and a bucket shower... meaning I'm just a simple girl, making the best of an excessively material world.

What was the motivation behind starting your business?
I needed to work for a company I believed in, and I wanted to commit as much time as I could to raising my daughter.

Tanya McLean

Anne Miller

𝒬 and 𝒜

What are the most popular or best selling products or services?
Women's fashion, fabrics for wall hangings, bags, and bedding.

People may be surprised to know...
Although fifty years old, Marimekko is still one of the most influential leaders of modern fabric and clothing design in Europe.

What was the inspiration behind starting your business?
The incredible designs and colours of the products, the fashion collections offered, and the positive energy and direction of the head office in Helsinki.

Who is your role model or mentor?
My dear mother!

Where is the best place to find gifts?
Yaletown, and places I travel to.

Modern. Colourful. Bold.
Marimekko Vancouver is the first Concept Store in Canada for Marimekko of Finland. Marimekko brings happiness to people's everyday lives through colourful vibrant fabrics and modern fashion. The store offers a large collection of women's fashions from Marimekko's award-winning designers. There are also clothes for children and men, products for the bedroom, bathroom, and kitchen, and colourful bags. Bolts of Marimekko fabrics are available for drapes, wall hangings, and upholstery. Everything is manufactured by Marimekko, and originates from the amazing fabric designs that Marimekko continues to create.

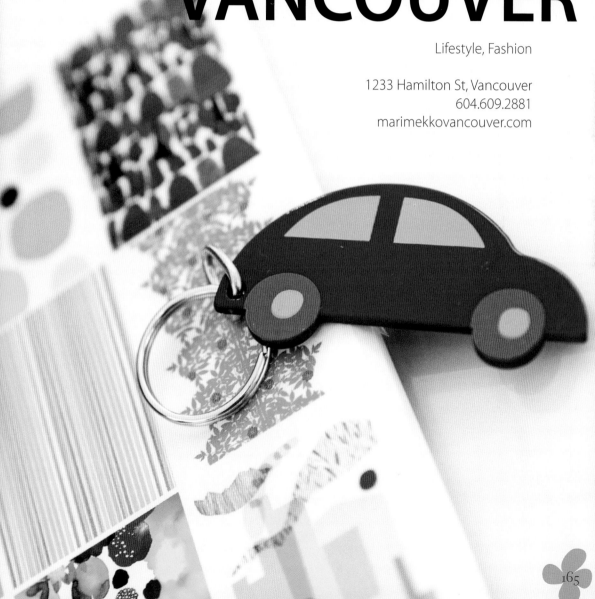

MARIMEKKO VANCOUVER

Lifestyle, Fashion

1233 Hamilton St, Vancouver
604.609.2881
marimekkovancouver.com

MARKUS J HAIR & WELL-BEING

Salon

2567 W Broadway, Vancouver
604.731.8383
markusjhair.com

Luxurious. Pampering. Trendy.

Markus J Hair and Well-Being, in the heart of Kitsilano, believes in inspiring men and women of all ages and ethnicities to take control of their hair! Let their experts help you find that cut and colour, customized to your individual look and personality. Indulge in total pampering, from signature facials to luxurious hair and scalp treatments. Private hair workshops, bridal services, extensions, and make-overs are Markus J's specialties!

How do you spend your free time?
Quality time with my two children, family, swimming, motivational seminars, and giving back by volunteering.

What is your indulgence?
Scones with lots of Devonshire cream, and a cup of tea!

What are the most popular or best selling products or services?
Japanese Gloss Treatment, Eminence Skin Care, Bumble and bumble "Straight," Rene Furterer "Melaleuca" anti-dandruff Shampoo.

People may be surprised to know...
That we hold private, one-on-one hair styling lessons and girlfriends hair workshops.

Where is the best place to buy clothes?
Japan. Or Florence, Italy.

Mona Leung

167

MASIK

Artist

Studio Visit by Appointment Only
info@masik.ca
masik.ca

Passionate. Innovative. Inspiring.

Masik manages and sells the exclusive collection of original Pamela Masik paintings to private and corporate collectors worldwide. While Pamela specializes in larger-scale paintings, she creates more accessible pieces that are available on her website. The company also books and produces exclusive performances by the artist. The Masik Foundation recently launched an e-commerce site for collectors to support community-based programs with a focus on a Social Arts Initiative to empower others in less fortunate circumstances. The photos on these pages will be featured in the about-to-be-released book of photography, an eight-year collaboration between Masik and Gordan Dumka.

 Q and A

How do you spend your free time?
Breathing in the ocean air, observing the changing seasons, watching a ball game with my son, exploring the world, giving back to the community, laughing a lot and embracing life.

What was the inspiration behind starting your business?
My son inspired me to be who I am and live a life of purpose, not just for myself but for him. He is truly the one who inspires me every day.

What are the most popular or best selling products or services?
My larger paintings are becoming well-collected and I often have a waiting list. I find the more authentic the work is, I mean being true to my artistic expression, the more successful I am. On my website, I recently launched a collection that is more accessible to young collectors who would like to acquire fine art while helping others within their community.

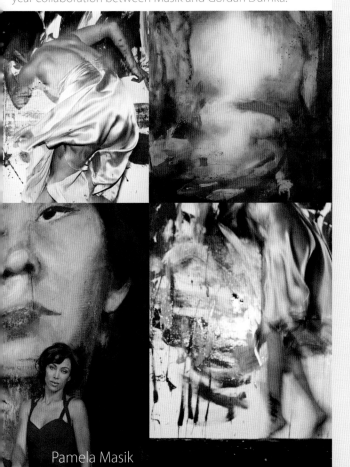

Pamela Masik

MAUDE SALON

Salon

2072 W 4th Ave, Vancouver
604.730.9933

What are the most popular or best selling products or services?
Our best selling product line would be Davines hair products. They manage to be environmentally conscious and work wonders on your hair. These to things are hard to find.

What was the inspiration behind starting your business?
I wanted to create a salon without attitude, where all clients felt welcomed not intimidated. An environment where the stylists felt appreciated, and a salon that felt like a small neighbourhood salon, but had the skills of a downtown salon.

Where is the best place to find gifts?
I live in Paboom on 4th. They are affordable, and have a great mix of items. We always get window display ideas there.

Friendly. Genuine. Creative.

Maude is a small boutique salon in the heart of Kitsilano. The shop is modern and cutting-edge, yet maintains a friendly neighbourhood atmosphere. The stylists at Maude not only specialize in both cut and colour, they are also well known for their wedding styling. To complete your look, Maude offers hair products from around the world, and accessories from local designers.

Dani Hanson

171

Who is the best local designer?

"All designers who have the guts to pursue their dreams are the best in my mind."

Leighann Boquist, Oliver & Lilly's

Sherri Koop
Photography

The Megahair Family
Misch Shop
MoBoleez
Momcafé
Nima'ma
Nouvelle Nouvelle
Oliver & Lilly's
Portobello West
Pure Nail Bar
Rock.Paper.Scissors Inc.
Schaart Clothing Co.
The Secret Garden
 Tea Company
Sherri Koop Photography

THE MEGAHAIR FAMILY

Salon

Visit website for locations
604.599.6800
megahairfamily.com

Innovative. Charitable. Trend-Setting.

The Megahair Family consists of three distinct brands:

1. Megahair Salons. Oh-so-stylish hair combined with affordability and a vast variety of pro tools and products to shop from.

2. The award-winning, chic Zennkai Salon brand is Vancouver's answer to the coveted "my-hair-just-does-this" style. Carrying over 70 professional hair product brands at amazing prices.

3. Boutique-inspired Eccotique delivers on high expectations in both hair and spa services. It is a fashionista's paradise with brands like Kerastase, Bumble and bumble, Aveda, Bliss, Cargo, and Frederic Fekkai.

Milajne Soligo

Q and A

What was the inspiration behind starting your business?
Providing our guests salons and spas that can be enjoyed everyday, not just as a luxury once a year, in environments that are both comfortable, fun, and contemporary!

People may be surprised to know...
I use to live in Croatia when I was little.

What is your indulgence?
Food - especially ice cream with hot fudge and nuts!

What mistake have you made in your business that you will not repeat?
I just believe in being a student for life. There are always learning lessons and opportunities that push me to be better everyday.

How do you spend your free time?
I read tons of books and I love hiking.

MISCH SHOP

Fashion

2960 Granville St, Vancouver
604.731.1017
misch.ca

Unique. Feminine. Modern.

A charming boutique on stylish South Granville, Misch is a delicious blend of hard-to-find labels and emerging designers, a perfect treat for every woman with a craving for fashion. Owner Lara Osen, has a natural penchant for what is both current and cutting-edge. With a focus on little-known lines such as Loeffler Randall and Hanni Y, as well as indie favourites like Vanessa Bruno and Isabel Marant, Lara has managed to create the atmosphere of a New York boutique in the heart of South Granville.

 Q and A

What is the best gym or fitness club?
I go with my dog to the trails at UBC, or Spanish Banks at low tide.

People may be surprised to know...
That we have a little secret garden behind the store.

How do you spend your free time?
With my wonderful daughter!

What was the motivation behind starting your business?
My dad always said that he jumped out of bed each morning, excited to start the work day. I wanted (and found) a job that I felt the same passion for.

Where is your favourite place to go with your girlfriends?
My front porch with prosecco, olives and lots of laughter.

Lara Osen

Q and A

What are the most popular or best selling products or services?
Our most popular design has a bunny sipping a coffee that says "Cafe Au Lait" on the top of the head - very French looking, and so cute! Another popular design is our "Milky Way" hat - great for little astronomer babies!

People may be surprised to know...
I have no background in garment design or fashion! I knew next-to-nothing about manufacturing before I started this venture. I had to rely on my ability to ask a lot of questions and find the right people to help me.

What mistake have you made in your business that you will not repeat?
Not doing a credit check on people who ask to "pay later." What does it say on the US dollar bill? "In God we Trust," so all others pay up-front or send me your credit info!

Diane Sam

Unique. Innovative. Fun.
MoBoleez designs, markets, and sells innovative products that celebrate the nursing mom in fun and stylish ways. Owner Diane Sam has created the world's first breast-feeding hat, which is patent pending, and has been well received by press, moms, and retailers. MoBoleez hats are sold in quality gift/baby shops worldwide - over 100 stores and growing!

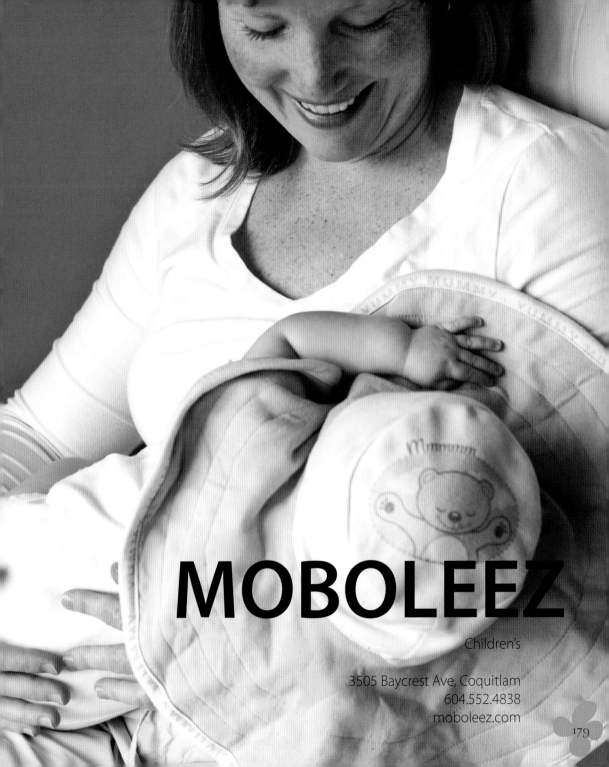

MOBOLEEZ

Children's

3505 Baycrest Ave, Coquitlam
604.552.4838
moboleez.com

Q and A

What was the inspiration behind starting your business?
WOMEN - The need for professional women who start having a family later in life, to come together to share ideas and support each other to do it all, whatever that may be!

What are the most popular or best selling products or services?
Event tickets and memberships. Who doesn't want to be inspired and connect with other like-minded women?

People may be surprised to know...
Jill sustains herself on coffee, chocolate, and wine!

What mistake have you made in your business that you will not repeat?
Trying to do too much with too little time!

Hilary Wooller and Jill Earthy

Inspiring. Educational. Fun.
Momcafé connects and inspires moms through monthly meetings and quarterly seminars, where women can learn from experts and each other about family and career, while benefitting from on-site childcare. Momcafé's online resources and membership provide valuable information and new connections, so that moms can choose the best path for now and in the future. Events currently run throughout the Lower Mainland and soon nationally.

MOMCAFÉ

Networking

PO Box 71090, 3553 W 41st Ave, Vancouver
604.787.5975
momcafe.net

NIMA'MA

Fashion

2938 W 4th Ave, Vancouver
604.734.8800
nimama.ca

Who is your role model or mentor?
I've always looked up to and admired my aunt, who is a successful interior designer and who has a brilliant, creative perspective and a tenacious and loving spirit. She has always been supportive of my ideas and personal endeavours.

What mistake have you made in your business that you will not repeat? Mistakes, I've made many. But I will say this to new retail owners: take your leasehold improvement budget and DOUBLE IT!

People may be surprised to know... Nima'ma hosts frequent - and free - breast-feeding and nutrition workshops in the boutique for expecting moms in an interactive, welcoming and informative two-hour session presented by Cherish Childbirth Care.

Friendly. Beautiful. Versatile.

Nima'ma is a women's apparel and accessories boutique in Kitsilano that specializes in quality maternity lines such as Jules & Jim, Boob, Olian, and Belabumbum; as well as non-maternity, luxurious, organic collections like Chloe Angus, Lav & Kush, Carol Young Undesigned and Nanna. The concept behind Nima'ma is to provide unique and versatile fashion options during maternity and beyond.

Teena Legris

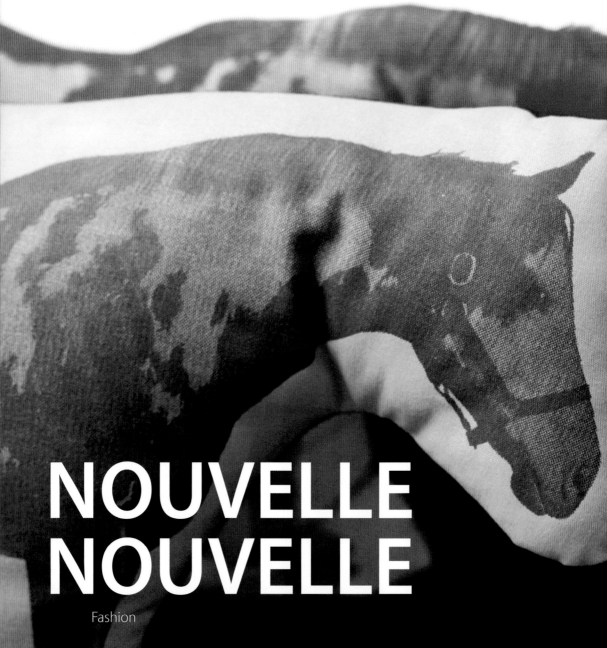

NOUVELLE NOUVELLE

Fashion

209 Abbott St, Vancouver
604.682.2234
nouvelle-nouvelle.com

Trendy. Funky. Fresh.

Nestled between cafés, restaurants, and art galleries along the cobblestone streets of Gastown, lies the chic boutique, Nouvelle Nouvelle. Offering a great variety of fashion-forward and often eco-conscious merchandise, it's a one-stop shop for fashionistas in Vancouver. The space is adorned with designs from the likes of Rowena Sartin, Samantha Pleet, and Velvet Leaf, along with great Canadian clothing designers, recycled leather bags, and one-of-a-kind jewellery.

Amy York

 Q and A

What was the motivation behind starting your business?
I decided to open Nouvelle Nouvelle to showcase some of the amazing independent lines that I loved but couldn't find in Vancouver at the time.

What are the most popular or best selling products or services?
Some of our current favourites include Mociun, Samantha Pleet, A Small Collection, Rowena Sartin, Permanent Vacation, Velvet Leaf, Manimal, Quail, Toujours Toi, Emily Katz, and Digby + Iona.

People may be surprised to know...
Gastown has always been my favourite part of the city, and I couldn't picture Nouvelle Nouvelle existing anywhere else. So, after almost a year of waiting and searching for the perfect space, I found it at 209 Abbott and opened in September 2007.

185

Q and A

What are the most popular or best selling products or services?
Our dresses and denim do fantastic for the women, and the vintage inspired basics line does amazing for the guys.

Who is your role model or mentor?
My parents! They are very hard-working, humble people. They always made my brother and I feel like we could do anything we set our minds to.

How do you spend your free time?
You can find me at home, sunk deep into my cozy couch, drinking tea, and reading magazines. I'm a home-body!

Where is the best place to get a pedicure?
Pure Nail Bar. It's such a fun environment to get your toes and hands pampered in. The bonus: they play Sex and The City episodes while you're getting primped.

Leighann Boquist

Imaginative. Charming.
Oliver & Lilly's is a cozy little neighbourhood boutique, obsessed with details and personality. Owner Leighann Boquist offers a magical and comfortable environment for both men and women to find clothing curiosities that are on trend, and casually classic. More than clothing, Oliver & Lilly's dabbles with fun home decor and accessories, just to keep the imaginative candle burning.

OLIVER & LILLY'S

PORTOBELLO WEST

Event

Rocky Mountaineer Station
1755 Cottrell St, Vancouver
778.855.2024
portobellowest.com

What are the most popular or best selling products or services?
Almost anything can be found at the market, from jewellery to original works of art. The options are limitless!

People may be surprised to know...
They can find high fashion from local designers, and that Vancouver is leading the way in eco-design.

What was the inspiration behind starting your business?
Portobello West was inspired by famous European markets like the Spitalfields in London.

Who is your role model or mentor?
I look up to leading entrepreneurs like Richard Branson, who listen to their customers and continue to innovate, no matter how big the business gets.

Original. Funky. Stylish.
Find your style and meet over 110 local artists and designers while you shop for one-of-a-kind fashion and art. Portobello West is held from noon to 6pm on the last Sunday of every month from March to November, with a holiday show two weeks before Christmas. Admission is only $2 (children 12 and under are free), and free parking and shuttle services are provided.

Carlie Smith

189

PURE NAIL BAR

Pamper

1282 Pacific Blvd, Vancouver
604.605.1282

2137 W 4th Ave, Vancouver
604.738.8990

991 Denman St, Vancouver
604.688.1866

3061 Granville St, Vancouver
604.730.1178

116 W 3rd St, North Vancouver
604.988.1150

4700 Kingsway Ave, Metropolis at Metrotown, Burnaby
604.439.7873

2267 W 41st Ave, Vancouver
604.263.9622

2836 Main St, Vancouver
604.874.9222

purenailbar.com

Pampering. Fun. Clean.

Pure Nail Bar is Vancouver's largest group of nail salon lounges, with seven popular locations. The latest location will be opening up this fall, in the fabulously revitalized Main Street neighbourhood. Whether you like getting pampered on your own, with a few girlfriends or celebrating in a large party, Pure Nail Bar is the perfect place to get your nails done!

Q and A

People may be surprised to know...
Unlike Pure Nail Bar, many nail salons actually reuse toe separators over and over again on many customers. Check if they rip open the individually packaged toe separators for you!

What is your indulgence?
Hair blowouts three times a week.

What was the inspiration behind starting your business?
It was not easy to find a stylish, fun, and clean nail salon that could accommodate a bunch of girlfriends, without paying high-end spa prices.

What mistake have you made in your business that you will not repeat?
Letting my husband pick out DVDs to play at the nail bar. He put on *The Godfather*!

How do you spend your free time?
Hanging out with my husband at our Whistler retreat.

Irene Lee

ROCK.PAPER. SCISSORS INC.

Event Services

laragan@rpsinc.ca
604.420.7703
rpsinc.ca

Strategic. Engaging. Illuminating.
More than 16 years and many awards later, Rock.
Paper.Scissors Inc. delivers incisive and interactive
training, team building, and entertainment
services to both large and small businesses,
locally and internationally. Combining training
expertise and professional improv comedians, RPS
workshops are sure to make you laugh (humor
is a terrific gateway to learning), learn (soak up
cutting edge knowledge), and lead (learn how
to take action and implement new skills).

 Q and A

Lee-Anne Ragan

What are the most popular or best
selling products or services?
Working Better Together (learn
techniques that foster responsiveness
and innovation to support team
building and communication),
"Train the Trainer" (helps people
who are experts in their context
become experts at teaching and
training), "Eight Lenses Individual
Assessment Tool" (a group
workshop that facilitates personal
performance and team effectiveness),
and Corporate Entertainment
Improv Comedy Services.

What is your indulgence?
Meditating at the Buddhist
temple, burlesque aerobics,
and creating moments of quiet
and stillness in my home.

193

Q and A

What are the most popular or best selling products or services?
My "Bon Bon" dress is available in ever-changing colours and prints and can be worn for any occasion.

People may be surprised to know... I used to work in an accounting office - the total opposite of the creative life I live now.

Where is the best place to buy shoes?
Fluevog in Gastown. I'm working down my wish list, shoe by wonderful shoe, boot by luscious boot!

How do you spend your free time?
Knitting, playing guitar and sketching new designs... or is sketching classified as work? Such a fine line!

Cheryl Densky

Classy. Modern. Sexy.
Vancouver designer Cheryl Densky combines her love of classic styles and textured fabrics to create interesting, wearable clothing for women in a full size range of 2 to 24. Schaart's clothing consists of modern, sophisticated classics with fine texture and exquisite tailoring. Must-haves include versatile shirtdresses, jersey knit dresses, topcoats for everyday living, and classic blouses with stretch featuring 3/4 length sleeves and decadent French cuffs.

194

SCHAART
CLOTHING CO.

Fashion

Visit website for nearest retailer
604.767.4554
schaartclothingco.com

195

Q and A

What are the most popular or best selling products or services?
Creamy Earl Grey Tea, Tiny Lemon Tarts and High Tea.

People may be surprised to know...
That we do catering!

What was the motivation behind starting your business?
My beautiful grandmother, who complained that there was nowhere to go for tea in Kerrisdale.

What mistake have you made in your business that you will not repeat?
Selling wedding cakes.

How do you spend your free time?
With our kids!

Who is your role model or mentor?
Ruby and Gina

Kathy and Erin Wyder

vanilla ROOIBOS tea

Warm. Comforting. Beautiful.
You can find The Secret Garden Tea Company in Kerrisdale, a village-like community nestled in the heart of Vancouver. When you enter The Secret Garden Tea Company, you will receive a warm welcome from one of their delightful shopgirls. The cozy establishment offers comfy seating, perfect for enjoying their afternoon tea, breakfast, lunch, or beautiful homemade miniature sweets or scones. An extensive variety of specially blended teas served steaming hot in a teacup and saucer are available for you to choose from. Secret Garden Tea Company is truly an experience: an urban oasis unlike any other!

THE SECRET GARDEN
TEA COMPANY

Eats, Event Services

5559 West Blvd, Vancouver
604.261.3070
secretgardentea.com

SHERRI KOOP
PHOTOGRAPHY

Photography

#202-70 E 2nd Ave, Vancouver
778.861.5667
sherrikoop.com

198

Life's Moments Captured.

Photographing stores of life and love is truly Sherri Koop's passion. Her intuitive photographic style results in images that are timeless and alive with emotion. She features individually hand-crafted presentation boxes, that combine modern design with unparalleled elegance.

Q and A

What are the most popular or best selling products or services?
Fine art canvas prints and handcrafted, silk presentation boxes.

People may be surprised to know...
That I actually like the rain!

What mistake have you made in your business that you will not repeat?
Thinking that I can be all things to all people.

How do you spend your free time?
Reading and writing.

What is your indulgence?
J. Crew cashmere.

What was the inspiration behind starting your business?
The birth of my first son.

Sherri
Koop

199

What is your indulgence?

"*Purses! I'm a hopeless pursaholic. Coach, vintage, or anything that catches my eye.*"

Patricia Harold, Studio 96 Designs

Shop Cocoon
Simply Sublime
Skindulgence
Skoah & Chiiki Munki
Skyler
Stonz Wear
Studio 96 Designs
The Style Spy
Sweet LeiLani Colour
  Cosmeceuticals
Tutta Mia
Urbane Decor
Urbanity
Valley of the Dolls
Vetrina Moda
Wonderbucks Trading
  Company
Y.E.S! Vancouver
Zing Paperie & Design

Valley of the Dolls

Q and A

People may be surprised to know...
All designers are intimately involved in the day-to-day running of the boutique, thus giving customers the rare opportunity to meet the designer on any given day.

Who is your role model or mentor?
My mom. She's every woman!

What mistake have you made in your business that you will not repeat?
I wouldn't change a thing.

How do you spend your free time?
Hiking, yoga, shopping.

What is your indulgence?
Shoes and coats.

Where is your favourite place to go with your girlfriends?
Savary Island Pie Co.

Brenda Li

Innovative. Creative. Unique.
Born with the vision of providing local designers, artists, and entrepreneurs with a platform to showcase their talents, Shop Cocoon has quickly grown to house 25+ different labels under one roof. Embracing the spirit, authenticity, and experimentalism of independence, Shop Cocoon's handpicked designers collectively deliver the finest in local design. Generating quite the stir in the fashion community, check out what's buzzing about Vancouver's destination store for a truly unique shopping experience.

SHOP COCOON

Fashion

3345 Cambie St, Vancouver
778.232.8532
shopcocoon.com

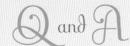

Q and A

Constantina "CJ" James

What are the most popular or best selling products or services?
Simply Sublime's real gold-dipped leaf jewellery.

What mistake have you made in your business that you will not repeat?
Spending too much money too fast.

How do you spend your free time?
Gardening, walking my dog Coco, reading fashion magazines.

People may be surprised to know...
I have my FAC (Firearms Acquisition Certificate), so I know how to handle and shoot any firearm!

What was the motivation behind starting your business?
I was unable to find quality, funky jewellery that didn't give my skin a reaction.

Upscale. Fashion Foward. Glamourous.
Simply Sublime is a local jewellery line created by Constantina "CJ" James. CJ's inspiration comes from her homeland, Greece, as well as New York City and Los Angeles. Stars like Jennifer Aniston and Britney Spears have been seen wearing Simply Sublime. CJ's jewellery company has now evolved to carrying high end clothing lines like Rich & Skinny, Velvet, and more. With this new found success, she was able to open a new Simply Sublime store with the help of a partner, Michaela Negrin, in Fall 2008.

SIMPLY
SUBLIME

Jewellery

#150-3737 Oak St, Vancouver
604.733.0440
simplysublime.ca

SKINDULGENCE
THE URBAN RETREAT

Pamper

254A Newport Dr, Newport Village, Port Moody
604.469.2688
skindulgencespa.com

Tranquil. Escape. Relaxed.

Skindulgence is an elite day spa that blends sophistication with tranquility. Owner Tazeem Jamal's key values are passion, people, and professionalism. She has been pampering the community for almost 20 years. Breathe Spa's holistic approach to skin care and well-being incorporates noninvasive anti-aging products and services. Tazeem believes serious skin care is a non-negotiable necessity. "Your skin is the largest organ of your body. What did you feed your skin today?"

Q and A

People may be surprised to know... As much as I am a social butterfly, I love quiet time at home in my PJ's!

What was the motivation behind starting your business?
Not to have to answer to anyone but myself, and the freedom to create my own successful future.

Who is your role model or mentor?
My best friend and confidante, my mom, Nazira. She has always believed in me, and always told me to follow my heart.

What is your favourite salon?
My girlfriend cuts my hair at home, and we get to visit at the same time!

What is your indulgence?
A great massage, amazing dark chocolate, and shoes. I'm secretly "Emelda in training!"

Tazeem Jamal

207

 # Q and A

Who is your role model or mentor?
My parents, for their kindness and truly generous hearts. My son, for reminding me of the importance of the simple things in life. My husband, for helping me achieve success in many areas of my life.

What mistake have you made in your business that you will not repeat? Doubting my gut instinct, allowing myself to feel intimidated or overwhelmed by others.

What is your indulgence?
Magazines of all kinds. They are stacked beside and under my bed.

Where is your favourite place to go with your girlfriends?
Whistler for a night away, or Seattle.

What is the best gym or fitness club?
The trails at UBC. That's my happy place.

Andrea Scott

years wi...
massage will h...
newlywed.

skoah.®
personal training for your skin

208

Simply Powerful Skin Care.
Skoah is a skin care specialty shop that exists to make you feel great from the skin in. Owner Andrea Scott offers simple skin care products, and delivers customized skin care workouts. Learn how you can have better skin with their personal skin care training lessons. In December 2007, Andrea launched an in-house makeup line, Chiiki Munki. It is easy to use, made of skin-caring ingredients, and was created to give busy people a few products, tips, and tricks to look great and feel fantastic!

SKOAH AND CHIIKI MUNKI

Pamper

1011 Hamilton St, Vancouver
604.642.0200

Metropolis at Metrotown
#314-4800 Kingsway, Burnaby
604.433.0200

Chinook Centre
#159-6455 MacLeod Trail SW, Calgary
403.203.0200

skoah.com
chiikimunki.com

209

Q and A

People may be surprised to know...
Our clothing fits exceptionally
well on ALL body types: big, small,
or pregnant. We don't put elastic
bands in the top of our pants, so
nobody needs to fear that they
will get the dreaded "muffin top!"

What was the motivation behind
starting your business?
We wanted to feel like we were
in our pajamas all day, but look
stylish enough to be seen in public!
That was the premise behind the
brand, comfortable clothing that
was still stylish and fashionable.

What mistake have you made in your
business that you will not repeat?
We think everything happens for a
reason. Like all new businesses, we
have made mistakes in the past, but
we feel like it is those mistakes that
has gotten us to where we are today.

Feminine. Stylish. Comfortable.
Skyler is a Vancouver-based fashion brand
focused on creating clothing that makes women
look and feel good all the time. Every garment
is made with the vision of combining fashion
and style, with comfort and practicality. Still
the best place to get feminine, sophisticated,
quality-fitting, street and active-wear, Skyler
dress-wear is now also a must-have!

Sky and
Christina Marcano

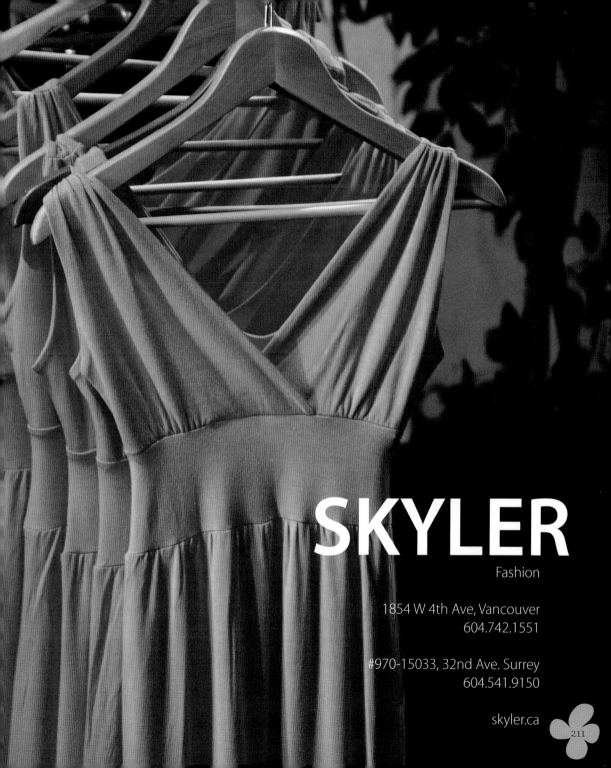

STONZ WEAR

Children's

604.568.6364
stonzwear.com

Innovative. Stylish. Canadian-Made.
Stonz creates innovative, versatile, and fashionable infant/toddler booties. The booties were born out of necessity to be outdoors with kids and have their feet remain warm. The booties are easy to put on, stay on, custom fit, wind/water resistant, and easily cared for. All of Stonz Wear's booties are made in Canada, as Owner Lisa Will feels strongly about supporting and promoting Canada's economy. Lisa is focused on what brings value to the customer; strong service and high quality, useful products.

What are the most popular or best selling products or services?
Baby booties in any form of brown; polka dots, stripes, bears, and cows.

What was the motivation behind starting your business?
Filling a need to keep little feet, aged newborn to 2, warm. Spending a lot of time outdoors with young babies and toddlers was difficult due to a lack of warm footwear that stayed on. We saw the need and filled it.

Where is your favourite place to go with your girlfriends?
Chocoholic bar at the Sutton Place Hotel; dessert and wine!

What is the best gym or fitness club?
Bentall Centre for kickboxing is a great stress reliever. The problem is, by the time you leave and drive home over a lined-up Lion's Gate Bridge, you're stressed all over again!

Lisa Will

STUDIO 96
DESIGNS

Event Services

429 Sherbrooke St, New Westminster
778.838.4024
studio96designs.com

Elegant. Simple. Romantic.
Studio 96 Designs is a one-stop location for brides to plan the decorative and floral elements for their special day. In a relaxed studio atmosphere, brides can see, touch, and try out the details that will bring their vision to life. Owner Patricia Harold's attention to detail will ensure all your needs are addressed, so you can celebrate stress free.

 Q and A

Patricia Harold

People may be surprised to know...
I'm working on designs for a line of cosmetic/travel bags.

What was the motivation behind starting your business?
Having my own venture where I could create freely, and follow my own path, instead of someone else's.

Where is your favourite place to go with your girlfriends?
The Secret Garden in Vancouver. They have a high tea that is truly incredible, and indulgent.

What are the most popular or best selling products or services?
Although I'm an event decorator, I seem to gravitate more toward weddings; both the decorating and the floral aspect.

215

Join the hottest style community in the city!

Get your backstage pass
Access!

the stylespy.com

THE STYLE SPY

Media

604.728.6488
thestylespy.com
contact@thestylespy.com

Creative. Growing. Charming.
Started in 2006, The Style Spy website
is the everyday girl's guide to shopping.
The Style Spy is your daily fix on fashion,
style, beauty, and sales. The Style Spy
is like that in-the-know girlfriend who
gives you the inside scoop on the new
boutique that just opened, the must-have
mascara, or that secret sample sale.

 Q and A

What is your indulgence?
Ferrero Rocher gelato at Mondo
Gelato, nail polish, and Sex and
the City DVD marathons.

Where is your favourite place
to go with your girlfriends?
Hapa Izakaya on Robson Street
for Japanese Tapas, Caffe Barney
on South Granville for eggs benny
or a trip to New York City!

People may be surprised to know...
That I don't shop 24/7! It takes
many long hours to run a great
website and business.

What was the inspiration behind
starting your business?
I wanted fashion and style to
be accessible to everyone. We
call our readers everyday girls.
We're not afraid to dish about
the $15 top we just bought or
shop designer discount!

Erica Lam

217

Q and A

What are the most popular or best selling products or services?
Studio Cover Stick Foundation, Lip and Cheek Tint, Pressed Mineral Powders.

People may be surprised to know...
LeiLani is also a hair stylist.

Where is your favourite place to go with your girlfriends?
Our own Beauty Box Central, a venue where girlfriends come and play at our makeup bar.

What mistake have you made in your business that you will not repeat?
Hiring representatives through brokerage companies rather than personally hiring our own team.

Pure. Natural. Beauty.
Sweet LeiLani Colour Cosmeceuticals is the first complete skin-care cosmetic line that is a better solution for sensitive, intolerant, and special skin, or for those simply looking for higher quality beauty products. LeiLani, a film industry artist could not find existing products to fill her needs, so she joined forces with her sister Tana, and they entered their first entrepreneurial venture. Sweet LeiLani Colour Cosmeceuticals is available at Pharmasave and Save-On Foods.

LeiLani Kopp and Tana McNicol

218

SWEET LEILANI
COLOUR COSMECEUTICALS

Pamper

#8-6280 202 St, Langley
778.896.4891
sweetleilani.com

Q and A

What are the most popular or best selling products or services?
Kairos Handbags, Fidelity Denim, Personal Styling, Togs, Precocious, and Gilmour.

What was the inspiration behind starting your business?
A desire to create a store that catered to local designers, and provided solutions for women who want to dress fashionably, but classically.

Who is your role model or mentor?
My husband has encouraged and inspired me to achieve everything that I have accomplished. His business background combined with a creative flair has been instrumental in my success.

What is your indulgence?
Living life to its fullest. Travel.

Gail Conzatti

Canadian. Personalized. Contemporary. Tutta Mia is the destination for women searching for Canadian and locally made clothing and accessories. Featuring elusive designers, customers are able to find unique pieces at Tutta Mia. Owner Gail Conzatti strives to provide fashionable, flattering styles that transition through several seasons.

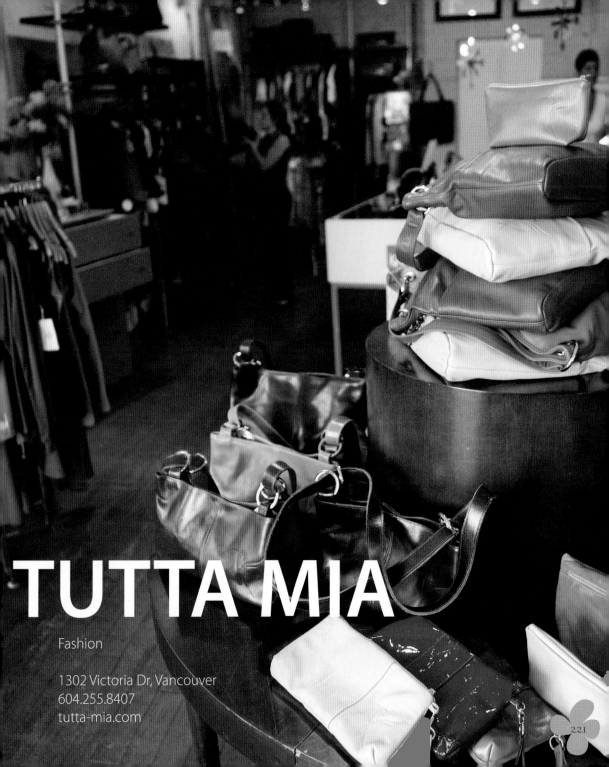

TUTTA MIA

Fashion

1302 Victoria Dr, Vancouver
604.255.8407
tutta-mia.com

Laura Davis

Q and A

People may be surprised to know...
How effective staging really is. You
want your home to be memorable
so it will stand out in a crowd.

What was the motivation behind
starting your business?
To be able to have a job I
am passionate about and
get paid to do it.

What mistake have you made in your
business that you will not repeat?
To ALWAYS have a written agreement
in hand before getting into any
business venture or contract.

What is your favourite salon?
Phenomenon in South Surrey.
Chau is my hairstylist. I don't take
any risks with my fine, fly-away
blond hair, and he really gets that.

Transformative. Innovative. Affective.
Urbane Decor helps sell houses faster - and at
premium prices. Laura Davis takes the stress out
of the process of getting your home ready to
sell. Her service packages range from vacant to
semi-vacant staging, and each job is specifically
tailored to your needs. The result: your home
is filled with life. Buyers no longer see empty
or half-put-together rooms needing touch up
paint, but instead imagine themselves relaxing
with friends and family. They fall in love with the
home, and make an offer you can't refuse.

222

URBANE DECOR

Stylist

#202-15388 24th Ave, South Surrey
604.720.6676
urbanedecor.com

223

URBANITY

Fashion

207 Abbott St, Vancouver
604.801.6262
urbanity.ca

Timeless. Beautiful.

Owner Julia Manitius moved to Vancouver in 2004 after living in Denmark for 28 years. Urbanity is Julia's first retail venture, as her background consists of teaching and creating. Julia and her products tell a story. Urbanity is about colour, quality, and natural materials, featuring a beautiful collection of sweaters, coats, skirts, and blankets from Oleana of Norway. Clothing and accessories are sourced from small factories or studios in Scandinavia and British Columbia.

What are the most popular or best selling products or services?
Beautiful merino/silk cardigans and felted accessories made in B.C.

What was the inspiration behind starting your business?
I wanted to create an environment and sell beautifully-designed, and well-made clothing. It's been a life-long dream.

What is your indulgence?
I travel looking for interesting products. I am a one-woman, three-year-old shop, so travelling is a true indulgence at this time.

Who is your role model or mentor?
One of the owners of Oleana of Norway, Signe Aarhus. She is soft, gentle, and idealistic, and has built a very successful business.

Julia Manitius

Q and A

What are the most popular or best selling products or services?
Crayola-coloured skinny jeans, silk floral A-line dresses, and tweed rompers.

What was the inspiration behind starting your business?
We're both heavily inspired by vintage design. We've combined the past with the present, offering up a modern vintage feel to the store.

Who is your role model or mentor?
My mother. She has always made me feel as though I can achieve anything I set my sights on.

People may be surprised to know...
We have a fabulous rack of designer vintage, as well as greatly edited non-label vintage.

Zrinka Domic

Avril Tait

Elegant. Feminine. Inspired.
Valley of the Dolls is Vancouver's latest go-to spot to find the freshest fashion obsessions at an incredible deal. The shop itself is airy and elegant, and has the ambience of your favourite mod lounge. If only there was a bar!

VALLEY OF THE DOLLS

Fashion

4332 Main St, Vancouver
604.569.3655
votdboutique.com

Rachel
Kapsalis

Q and A

People may be surprised to know...
That an independent boutique
has such a selection of exclusive
designers. We carry Paciotti
and Zaniotti shoes up to size
12, and some of our designer
fashions up to size 24!

What was the motivation behind
starting your business?
I have always enjoyed fashion,
travel, and working with people!

How do you spend your free time?
Cooking for friends and family.

What is your indulgence?
Tango classes!

Where is the best place
to get a pedicure?
For thorough, no-frills treatment,
I see Simon at Sukhis. When I
have time to relax, I see Jelena
at La Raffinage, and for cheap
and cheerful I go to Pro Nails.

Elegant. Addictive. Exclusive.
Vetrina Moda offers business wear and haute
couture, designer shoes and accessories, bath
and body products. Owner Rachel Kapsalis invites
you to experience European designer fashions
in her elegant, salon-style boutique. Each piece
has been hand-picked in Italy. With exclusive
European fashion lines, gowns by Jenny Packham,
Paciotti and Zanotti shoes, personal consultations,
very feminine plus sizes, and complimentary
refreshments, it's easy to see why The Vancouver
Sun has called Vetrina "the best kept secret in town."

VETRINA MODA

Fashion

525 W Georgia St, Vancouver
604.632.0132
vetrina.ca

WONDERBUCKS
TRADING COMPANY

Lifestyle

1803 Commercial Dr, Vancouver
604.261.0664
wonderbucks.ca

Cheap. Chic. Home.

Wonderbucks is different kind of home store. With inventory changing weekly, and sticker-shock pricing, owner Frances Blazich has, over the past 10 years, carved out a place that is a must-stop shop for Vancouverites. From furniture to kitchen, garden to art, and everything in between, Wonderbucks has something to amaze you.

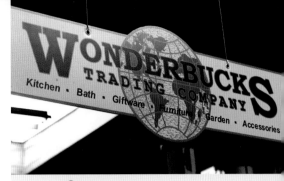

Frances Blazich

Q and A

What are the most popular or best selling products or services?
Decorative accessories and unusual gifts, but you have to be quick and come often!

How do you spend your free time?
Raising my four-year-old daughter.

What is your indulgence?
Travelling the world and shopping.

Where is your favourite place to go with your girlfriends?
Girls' night out, dinner, gossip, and drinks, anywhere!

People may be surprised to know...
We are not a dollar store. They are always amazed at what they can buy for a few bucks.

What mistake have you made in your business that you will not repeat?
Listening to my husband!

Y.E.S! VANCOUVER

Networking

604.408.7923
yesvancouver.org

Q and A

What are the most popular or best selling products or services?
Friends of Y.E.S! enjoy the excitement of our high-profile galas, and the chance to connect at our smaller events.

People may be surprised to know...
Every penny goes directly to Dress for Success, helping disadvantaged women in the Lower Mainland take charge of their lives.

What was the motivation behind starting your business?
We wanted to breathe fresh air into Vancouver's networking scene while bridging business and philanthropy; to help women help other women.

Who is your role model or mentor?
Dress for Success clients. These women overcome challenging situations to become dynamic contributors to our community.

Fresh. Fun. Impactful.
Y.E.S! is a fresh approach to networking and fundraising in Vancouver. It's more than your typical networking group, it's a new spin on fundraising. It's an entirely different way to get involved. It's where business and philanthropy come to meet and mingle. Friends of Y.E.S! gain access to amazing networking and fashion events, while championing the mission of Dress for Success® Vancouver.

Katrina Carroll
Foster and
Louise Weston

ZING PAPERIE & DESIGN

Lifestyle

#60-323 Jervis St, Coal Harbour Seawall, Vancouver
604.630.1885
zingdesign.ca

Fresh. Unique. Chic.
Fine, fun, and fabulous stationery is what you'll find at Zing Paperie & Design, a one-of-a-kind paper store located directly on the seawall in picturesque Coal Harbour. This bright and airy boutique is filled with stylish, earth-friendly note cards, modern invitations, beautiful wrappings, handcrafted journals, and many other goodies that are sure to inspire.

Q and A

What are the most popular or best selling products or services?
Swarovski crystal pencils, cool magnets, and personalized stationery

What was the motivation behind starting your business?
I'm passionate about design, and I'm drawn to the beauty of paper and the possibilities of communicating and connecting through it.

How do you spend your free time?
Biking, losing myself in a good design book while drinking a great cup of coffee, and spending time with family and friends.

What is your indulgence?
A nice, flaky chausson aux pommes.

Where is the best place to find gifts?
Butter Baked Goods – who doesn't enjoy receiving a beautifully packaged delicious sweet treat?

(Owner Tiffany Barkman is not pictured)

Manifest

Artists
  Masik, 168

Children's
  Chick Pea, 52
  Hip Baby, 112
  Lola Home & Apparel, 150
  Mally Bibs, 160
  MoBoleez, 178
  Oliver & Lilly's, 186
  Stonz Wear, 212

Eats
  Butter Baked Goods, 44
  Domo Tea, 68
  Emelle's Catering, 80
  Little Nest, 146
  The Secret Garden
    Tea Company, 196

Event Services
  Emelle's Catering, 80
  The Finer Details, 96
  Make It Productions, 156
  Rock.Paper.Scissors Inc., 192
  The Secret Garden
    Tea Company, 196
  Studio 96 Designs, 214

Events
  Portobello West, 188

Eyewear
  Bruce Eyewear, 40
  Della Optique, 64

Fashion
  Adhesif Clothing Co., 10
  Alarte Silks, 12
  Babs Studio Boutique, 14
  Bare Basics, 18
  Bodacious Lifestyles, 34
  Bootyfly Bags/No BS Headband, 156
  Boudoir, 36
  Changes Clothing &
    Jewellery Bar, 50
  Dorothy Grant, 70
  Dream Apparel, 72
  Edie Hats, 76
  Enda B Men & Women, 82
  Favourite Gifts, 92
  Fine Finds, 94
  Flaming Angels Boutique, 100
  Gaya Canada Enterprise Ltd., 106
  Honey Love Design Boutique, 114
  Ishara, 122
  JC Studio, 126
  Kim Allan Silk, 136
  Larry Designs, 138
  Liquid, 142
  Lola Home & Apparel, 150
  M0851, 154
  Malary's Fashion Network, 158

Fashion (continued)
Marimekko Vancouver, 164
Misch Shop, 176
Nima'ma, 182
Nouvelle Nouvelle, 184
Oliver & Lilly's, 186
Schaart Clothing Co., 194
Shop Cocoon, 202
Skyler, 210
Tutta Mia, 220
Urbanity, 224
Valley of the Dolls, 226
Vetrina Moda, 228

Fitness
Burlesque Beauties, 42
Exhale Studio, 90

Floral
Academy of Floral Design
& New Westminster
Floral Company, 8

Jewellery
Blue Ruby Jewellery, 30
Changes Clothing
& Jewellery Bar, 50
Jeweliette, 128
Lolo Jewellery, 152
Simply Sublime, 204

Lifestyle
Bella Ceramica, 24
Country Beads, 56
The Cross Decor & Design, 58
Designhouse, 66
Dream Designs, 74
Favourite Gifts, 92
Front & Company, 104
Heather Ross [in house], 110
Lola Home & Apparel, 150
Marimekko Vancouver, 164
Wonderbucks Trading Company, 230
Zing Paperie & Design, 234

Media
Daily Dose Media, 62
Five Corners Media, 98
The Honey Mustard Fashion
& Media Services/Fashion High, 118
The Style Spy, 216

Networking
The Campoverde Social Club, 46
Forum for Women
Entrepreneurs (BC), 102
Loaded Bow, 148
Momcafé, 180
Y.E.S! Vancouver, 232

Manifest

Pamper
Absolute Spa Group, 6
Beautybar, 20
The BeautyInk Gallery, 22
Beverly's the Spa on 4th, 26
Bloom Essentials, 28
Breathe Spa, 38
Elements Wellness Centre, 78
Escents Aromatherapy, 84
EvelineCharles Salons & Spas, 86
Jag Dhahan, 124
Jo's Toes & Esthetics, 130
Le Petit Spa, 140
Pure Nail Bar, 190
Skindulgence, 206
Skoah & Chiiki Munki, 208
Sweet LeiLani Colour
   Cosmeceuticals, 218

Photography
Colektiv Images, 54
Höng Photography Studio, 120
Katwalk Photography, 134
Sherri Koop Photography, 198

Salons
EvelineCharles Salons & Spas, 86
Gloss Salon, 108
Markus J Hair & Well-Being, 166
Maude Salon, 170
The Megahair Family, 174

Shoes
Kalena's Italian Shoes
   & Accessories, 132

Stylists
Carrie & Danielle, 48
Mango Design Co, 162
Urbane Decor, 222

Technology
Backbone Systems, 16

the
CRAVEcompany™
Innovative Connections

The CRAVEcompany innovatively connects small business owners with the customers they crave. We bring together small business communities and fuel them with entrepreneurial know-how and fresh ideas - from business consulting to shopping fairs to new media. CRAVEcompany knows what it takes to thrive in the modern marketplace.

CRAVEmedia™
Style and Substance.
Delivered.

CRAVEmedia is the go-to resource for urban minded women. We celebrate stylish entrepreneurs by showcasing the most creative, interesting, and gutsiest proprietors from cities all over the world.

CRAVEbusiness™
A Fresh Approach to
Modern Business

CRAVEbusiness is a social, resource network for stylish innovators who own their own business, or dream of starting one. Through one-on-one consulting, workshops, and red-carpet access to sage and savvy experts, entrepreneurs meet with others in their fields to get a fresh approach to their business.

CRAVEparty®

What do You Crave?

"Everything you Crave" all under one roof.

CRAVEparty is an exclusive, festive, glam-gal gathering of fun, entertainment, personal pampering, specialty shopping, sippin' and noshin', and just hanging with the girls.

Indulge and splurge (you deserve it) on spa treatments, massages, manis and pedis, fashion shows, irresistible boutique shopping – all in a spirited, and carefree atmosphere.